Strategic Bootstrapping

Strategic Bootstrapping

Matthew W. Rutherford, Ph.D.

BUSINESS EXPERT PRESS

Strategic Bootstrapping
Copyright © Business Expert Press, LLC, 2015.

First published in 2015 by
Business Expert Press, LLC
222 East 46th Street, New York, NY 10017
www.businessexpertpress.com

ISBN-13: 978-1-60649-698-5 (paperback)
ISBN-13: 978-1-60649-699-2 (e-book)

Business Expert Press Babson College Entrepreneurship Research
Conference Collection

Collection ISSN: 2372-0492 (print)
Collection ISSN: 2372-0530 (electronic)

Cover and interior design by S4Carlisle Publishing Services Private Ltd.,
Chennai, India

First edition: 2015

10 9 8 7 6 5 4 3 2 1

Printed in the United States of America.

Abstract

This book is about helping entrepreneurs sift through the "noise" regarding bootstrapping a start-up. Ultimately, the cold-hard facts on bootstrapping will be presented. Practically speaking, most entrepreneurs should avoid bootstrapping. However, realistically, most entrepreneurs will need to engage in some form of bootstrapping. The argument then, importantly, shifts to how should one bootstrap? In this era of lean start-ups, effectuation, and bricolage, bootstrapping is oft romanticized but seldom analyzed. This book is different from other bootstrapping books in two key ways. First, it draws on evidence from scientific study to offer best practices. Second, it utilizes this evidence to help entrepreneurs thrive—not just survive.

Keywords

Bootstrapping, new venture strategy, new venture finance

Contents

CHAPTER 1

Bootstrapping Described

About This Chapter

New firms are different. Firms that are still in developmental infancy represent a distinct subsection of the universe of all firms. Indeed, experts have noted that new ventures differ fundamentally from more mature firms and these differences mean that new strategies and tactics must be developed, because strategies for survival and growth cannot simply be shipped wholesale from the realm of mature firms (McDougall & Robinson, 1990).

Consider, for example, Under Armour in 1995. Now a household name and wildly successful apparel firm, Kevin Plank started this company from his grandmother's garage and sold product out of his car. Since it took him over a year to land his first major account—a team sale to Georgia Tech—he had to live very frugally because initially no customers were willing to buy a fledgling product from a novice entrepreneur with a company that had no history or legitimacy. Because of this lack of legitimacy, he built his business on hustle and thrifty living.

New ventures like 1995 Under Armour lack financial, human, and social capital. They have no legitimacy, reputation, or status, and as a result face long odds competing with more established competitors who do not have this set of liabilities. As organizations mature, they gain unique resources and cultures that allow them to differentiate themselves from the competition (Barney, 1991). As a result of these issues, new ventures fail at a much higher rate than more mature ventures. While estimates vary, most would put the chances of surviving 3 years at about 60 percent, and closer to 50 percent at 5 years (Knaup, 2005).

The rate of success is likely lower for those entrepreneurs who decide to launch their firm with no outside financial assistance (Ranger-Moore, 1997). These so called bootstrappers are exacerbating their inherent disadvantages by limiting their access to financial capital. However, most entrepreneurs do bootstrap and some prosper. Kevin Plank founded his company's launch with credit cards, taking no equity finance or bank debt in the founding years.

Plank's success aside, after taking all the risk factors into account, it is a wonder that the failure rate for new firms is not much higher. How could any firm be expected to survive in such a harsh environment, with such substantial disadvantages? But many new firms, like Under Armour, do survive and some even grow, create jobs, and generate tremendous wealth for entrepreneurs.

It is the goal of this work to investigate ways that entrepreneurs can increase these survival rates and have a much greater chance to create wealth for themselves and others, even if they decide to eschew external financing. But, it is also the goal here to encourage entrepreneurs to think through the decision to bootstrap very carefully.

There has been an explosion of articles, books, blogs, etc. that all attempt to help entrepreneurs navigate this precarious stage of existence. Much of this writing is based on anecdotal evidence from the entrepreneur/author. This book takes a different approach to assist new venture entrepreneurs—it takes an evidence-based approach. That is, the research on the topic is reviewed and applied to the practice of starting the new venture. In addition to the wealth of knowledge available from practicing entrepreneurs, academics and other experts have collected and analyzed a large amount of data. The results of this analysis can add new and objective information that can assist the practitioner in decision making.

This is certainly not to suggest that the evidence-based approach is better than the anecdotal approach, but it is to suggest that one approach is not complete without the other. This book should be seen as a companion piece to the more anecdotal, personal experience-based books currently on the market (e.g., *The Art of the Start* by Guy Kawasaki). It is meant to provide objective facts to the entrepreneur, where those facts are available. In this book, we will drill down into the theory and evidence on one specific facet of the start-up—the process and content of bootstrapping.

What Is It?

Briefly, bootstrapping is understood as the condition whereby start-up entrepreneurs operate (often in creative ways) their firms with no outside financial assistance. This is certainly a condition in which many entrepreneurs find themselves, and there is little argument about that (Aldrich & Martinez, 2001; Shepherd & Zacharakis, 2003), but there are differing opinions regarding whether one should choose to bootstrap if given the choice. These opinions are often conflicting and therefore confusing. In carrying out the goals of the book, this advice will be organized and examined.

The practice of bootstrapping captures at least the following activities that arise from the entrepreneur's unwillingness or inability to attract external financing:

- Keeping one's day job to invest salary
- Utilizing home-equity
- Using credit cards
- Operating from home
- Sweat equity—working long hours
- Loans from family and friends

Avoiding outside investment makes it a virtual necessity that an entrepreneur will have to rely on these activities to stay afloat.

As noted there has been copious writing in the popular press on the topic of bootstrapping, but there has been a bit less in the realm of academia. Infamously deliberate with regard to publishing results, academics who research entrepreneurship are just now reaching a critical mass of research and writing on the topic.

Historically, the academic research on financing focused on the larger, older firm. Yet, as noted, new ventures have a significantly different set of opportunities and constraints than established businesses. For this reason, traditional theories and models of the firm sometimes have had difficulty translating to the new venture. Entrepreneurs are finding this research and teaching from business schools difficult to implement in their situations. Moreover, much of the academic writing on bootstrapping specifically has focused on small—not new—firms. As will be asserted throughout this book, the new firm is a different beast, not only different from large firms, but different from smaller, older firms as well.

Consider the apparel company, Gerbing's, when compared to a start-up like Under Armour. Headquartered in Stoneville, NC, Gerbing's manufactures heated clothing for hunters and other outdoor enthusiasts. The firm is almost 40 years old with 50 employees and $15 million in revenue—certainly small, but not new (Privco, n.d.). Practical advice given to a firm such as this would likely not have been overly helpful to Kevin Plank in his bootstrapped start-up—and vice versa. Frankly, the fundamentals of Gerbing's are far closer to a Fortune 500 firm than a start-up. For example, the managers of Gerbing's likely spend far more time making decisions about *managing* resources—that is, which employees to hire, which financing to accept, or which new plant to open—than about *attracting* initial customers and financing. These two types of firms are so different that they hardly resemble one another. As renowned economist, Edith Penrose states, "The differences in the administrative structure of the . . . [two] are so great that in many ways it is hard to see that the two species are of the same genus" (Penrose, 1959).

Building on this relatively new and growing base of research on the topic, this chapter introduces the notion and nuances of bootstrapping. It also introduces key concepts and relationships that will be referred to throughout this book.

The Cowboy Way—Brief History of Bootstrapping

To this writer's knowledge, the term *bootstrapping* originated in the cowboy lexicon as way of describing how cowboys would arise from a seated position to standing. They would reach down, grab the straps of their boots and rock to an upright position. In this way, the self-sufficient cowboy or cowgirl accomplished goals using only what was immediately available on their person—receiving no assistance from the outside. This metaphor has great appeal to the entrepreneurial community, as many entrepreneurs view themselves as renegades, mavericks, and/or lone-wolves, and so it persists.

Bootstrapping is often discussed, but rarely defined. Noted to be an, "essential entrepreneurial phenomenon" (Grichnik & Singh, 2010), bootstrapping is a term that has been discussed in the academic literature for at least 20 years, but has only recently received rigorous examination by scholars.

A review of the academic and popular press reveals multiple definitions of bootstrapping. Most incorporate the idea that bootstrapping is a process whereby entrepreneurs assemble resources and at least persevere—if not grow—without utilizing debt or equity financing from outside banks and/or investors. This process is generally termed *financial bootstrapping* (Freear, Sohl, & Wetzel, 1995). But, in actuality bootstrapping comprises two related, but distinct activities. To be complete, a definition should also address the fact that entrepreneurs must be imaginative to discover ways to compete and survive without access to this financing. As such bootstrapping is not only the absence of outside debt or equity, it is also the ongoing process of acquiring other resources (e.g., supplies, employees, equipment) at minimal cost (Freear, Wetzel, & Sohl, 1990).

Bootstrapping also presupposes that the entrepreneur brings a relatively limited amount of resources to the table. Present day Warren Buffet, for example, would likely do very well as the entrepreneur of a bootstrapped firm because, for all intents, his venture would not be bootstrapped. Mr. Buffet could bring his enormous personal wealth to internally finance his business. He, personally, has more wealth than most venture capital (VC) firms. Therefore, there would be little need for him to engage in creative tactics to operate in a frugal manner, even if he chooses to avoid external finance.

Bootstrapping is often discussed as inevitability in start-ups, as the refrain goes: "there is simply no money for aspiring entrepreneurs." And, on average, it is true that new businesses do not receive external funding and that new ventures have fewer financing options than more mature ventures. However, it is also the case that, as we stand in the afterglow of the Jumpstart Our Start-Ups (JOBS) Act, that there has never been a time when there were more options for external financing.

So, importantly, the primary cause of lack of external financing is not the so called "funding gap"—the reluctance on the part of financiers to lend to new ventures—it is because entrepreneurs do not ask for external funding (Shane, 2008). To be clear, even if they asked, many new venture entrepreneurs would likely still not receive financing, but far more would. This fact is the key and will be referred to throughout.

Because many entrepreneurs identify with the "cowboy way," there is a tendency, particularly in the popular press to glorify the bootstrapped entrepreneur, and with good reason. Any individual or team that can survive—or grow—without external money should be celebrated. Firms like Ben and Jerry's, Google, and Pandora were all bootstrapped and are very much celebrated.

But readers should understand that it is extremely difficult to simply survive without external funding and nearly impossible to grow. The role of the popular press is to celebrate the outliers—not to accurately describe the average, or most likely condition. Virtually all of the advice provided by expert entrepreneurs is correct, in that it reflects what worked for them in their specific context or contexts—war stories, if you will. The problem, though, is that one expert's advice often conflicts with another's and novice entrepreneurs get buried under an avalanche of conflicting advice. Throughout this book, I will attempt to provide clarity to this advice.

The reality is that bootstrapped entrepreneurs are likely to struggle to overcome the inherent burdens associated with being new (Neeley & Van Auken, 2010), and as a result, will fail. The only way to overcome these burdens is to be "old", or at least appear that way, and this usually requires resources.

Bootstrapping is an ironic concept. In one way, bootstrapping can be a very freeing experience. Free from external financiers, cowboy entrepreneurs are able to operate their businesses in the way that they choose—they have the much sought after autonomy. In another way, though, bootstrapping represents, by definition, constraint. Entrepreneurs are free to act however they wish within some fairly tight resource boundaries.

Therefore, this book encourages the entrepreneur to think through carefully what starting as a bootstrapper means. Specifically, the entrepreneur should think through ways that a start-up might achieve a large degree of autonomy, while simultaneously shedding some of the debilitating capital constraints. There are more ways to do this than one might think.

Bootstrapping Involves Making Choices about Initial Financing

So, entrepreneurs bootstrap for one, or both, of the following reasons: (1) the decision is made to eschew external financing, or (2) external financiers deny to provide such funding. The majority of entrepreneurs bootstrap (Kim et al., 2006), but their motivation for bootstrapping matters immensely. The end result is largely the same (i.e., financial constraint), but the process is important because some processes are much more likely to end in failure than others. If entrepreneurs are bootstrapping simply because they are driven by a desire for autonomy, control, or risk aversion; the prognosis is likely a bit better than if the entrepreneur is bootstrapping because he or she must. When an entrepreneur is denied funding by debt providers or financiers, this is a clear market signal that the firm is primed for failure (Carpentier & Suret, 2006). This is an important point: being denied financing is a feedback windfall for the entrepreneur. Stated differently, the decisions that financiers make about the viability of a new venture should be taken very seriously by entrepreneurs.

The popular press is full of examples of entrepreneurs who persisted through rejection after rejection from money handlers to eventually succeed, ostensibly because the financiers were dim. To be clear, this happens and financiers miss opportunities often. Moreover, many new ventures are simply not appropriate for funding. However, if funding is denied, it is also likely that the entrepreneur has either misidentified the opportunity or done a poor job of communicating its viability. Entrepreneurs must be very careful and honest with themselves if they decide to launch after being denied funding. The confidence (or overconfidence) that many entrepreneurs possess is likely critical for success, but this bias comes with a number of negatives that must be addressed (Cooper, 1988).

In general, firms with more resources on average increase their chances of survival and growth (Singh, Ang, & Leong, 2003). Acquiring resources is, virtually by definition, a method of shedding newness burdens. Building on this, simply by going through the process of requesting external funds, the entrepreneur builds social and human capital by receiving valuable information from knowledgeable stakeholders. There is value being added to the firm and the entrepreneur during the capital raising process, and it is far better to request funding early than to wait until a time when the entrepreneur is truly desperate. Financiers—particularly lenders—like to grant funding when entrepreneurs do not need it.

Bootstrapping Involves Creatively Operating in Resource-Poor Environments

Not only does an entrepreneur's motivation for bootstrapping matter, so too does the entrepreneur's strategy when bootstrapping. This second component of bootstrapping is even more involved than the first; for it involves the day-to-day tasks the entrepreneur must perform to survive with limited resources. As will be explored in this book, some of these are more fruitful than others.

The activities undertaken to survive in this resource-scarce environment are numerous and range from the obvious to the subtle. Delaying payments to suppliers is one obvious and quintessential example of bootstrapping. It is quintessential because it allows the entrepreneur to make use of some good or service for "free" until the entrepreneur pays the provider. Anyone who has paid their phone bill late is familiar with this technique. Another very common method is working part-time in the new business while working full-time in a different job. This allows entrepreneurs to subsidize the new business with income from their "day job," thereby allowing them to avoid external finance.

While most would agree that these techniques represent bootstrapping, few would agree that they are creative. There are, in fact, some relatively creative bootstrapping techniques and these tend to be more fruitful than those listed above. For example, sharing employees with a similar new firm has substantial advantages for the bootstrapper. It offers access to valuable human capital, it offers networking opportunities with the other business (i.e., social capital), and of course it is cheaper than employing the person with no assistance (i.e., financial capital).

Methods for sharing employees are numerous, but one general way to do this is to apply for space in an incubator or accelerator. Many locales now boast at least one of these entities that allow tenants to—not only share employees (e.g., secretarial and informational technology workers)—but also equipment and other resources. Another relatively novel way to share employees is by contracting with a "fractional chief financial officer." Fahrenheit Group in Richmond, Virginia, for example, is a firm that supplies talented CFO's to start-ups who cannot afford (and likely do not require) a full time CFO. These fractional officers will likely provide financial services for a number of start-ups.

In this way, sharing employees and employing fractional officers embraces the paradox of containing costs while growing the resource base. Clearly, these types of techniques are the most desirable and it is these techniques that strategic bootstrapping comprise. It is these techniques that this book will highlight.

Myths Associated with Bootstrapping

* Myth: There is no money available for start-ups.
  Reality: It is certainly challenging to attract funding at the start-up stage, but good ideas will attract funding—if the entrepreneur can communicate them effectively. A few examples of less celebrated sources are private investors, angel groups, crowdfunding, and micro-lending institutions. All of these sources provide much more capital to new ventures than one might think. While estimates vary, most experts believe that at least $30 billion per year is invested by these entities. This represents investments in approximately 30,000 ventures by 300,000 individuals (Sohl, 2003; Butler et al., 2013). Moreover, it is expected that these numbers will escalate quickly with the full passage of the JOBS Act.
  Entrepreneur Lidia Calzado faced a common new venture problem. She did not have enough funds to buy supplies in bulk; therefore her cost-per-unit was very high. This left her fledgling jewelry and perfume business with a very low profit margin. She applied for, and received, a $10,000 loan from micro-lending outfit ACCION, San Diego. This allowed her to substantially boost her profit margin by purchasing supplies at a lower per-unit rate (http://www.accion.org/page .aspx?pid=4326).

- Myth: Equity players will lock an entrepreneur into a course of action by not allowing that entrepreneur to change strategic direction when necessary or desired.

  Reality: The notion that an individual or entity would invest a large sum of money into a start-up and then resist important changes is difficult to support with logic. In the management literature, the notion of escalation of commitment is often used to describe a scenario whereby an individual continues to devote time and money to a course of action long after it is clear that this course of action is doomed. Rational players are less likely to succumb to this cognitive bias. A VC or angel with "skin in the game" is likely to support any change of direction that will increase viability of the new firm.

  Consider, for example, Marbles: The Brain Store. This venture launched as a kiosk-based retailer of puzzles, games, and software in 2008. After receiving funding from a Chicago-based VC firm, the business was floundering. The entrepreneur decided, with no apparent pushback from the VC, to rebrand the store so as to be more "hands on" and experimental so that customers could play the games. She also moved to a much more expensive and high traffic area. She now has 27 U.S. locations and employs 185 people, with annual revenue of approximately $20 million (http://www.entrepreneur.com/article/229372).

  Research on the topic in entrepreneurship actually supports the opposite condition—an entrepreneur without knowledgeable partners will be less likely to "pivot." This is based on the simple fact that entrepreneurs, probably more than any potential investor, are filled with biases and possibly the most pronounced is overconfidence (Cooper, 1988) that often manifests itself as stubbornness. This bias for entrepreneurs, albeit a necessary one, needs to be tempered with objective guidance from knowledgeable outsiders.

- Myth: Bootstrapping is less risky than using external finance.

  Reality: This is dependent on one's definition of "risk." It could certainly be argued that financing a start-up with 100 percent of the founder's money is more risky than, say

50 percent. Particularly if that money is being supplied in the form of equity—the investor shares the risk. Almost by definition, raising equity reduces the risk level of the entrepreneur. Moreover, as noted, it is generally true that firms started with less capital face higher failure rates. Here again, bootstrapping may result in elevated risk.

- Myth: Bootstrapping allows the entrepreneur to be autonomous. Reality: There is autonomy for entrepreneurs in that they will not have to consult other owners when making decisions. However, because bootstrapped entrepreneurs are likely resource constrained, they are more dependent on customers, suppliers, and other stakeholders, and must often go to great lengths to appease them. So, bootstrapped entrepreneurs do gain power in the ownership dimension, but likely lose in many other dimensions. A well-resourced start-up can dictate terms with stakeholders far more effectively.

  Eco-me is a company that resembles this. Founded in 2009, the company manufactures and sells all natural cleaning products. The company was bootstrapped by the founders (Robin Levine and Jennifer Mihajlov) and was achieving excellent top-line growth, but was not profitable. The duo had difficulty negotiating good terms with retailers and suppliers. On the supplier side, specifically, they needed new machinery to be able to grow the business. However, the machinery was too expensive and the cash-poor firm could not negotiate a favorable deal. In 2013, Eco-me received a substantial cash infusion by an angel investor. This allowed the company to purchase the machinery, rebrand the product, and professionalize the sales team. All of this resulted in tremendous sales growth (http://www.greencleaningmagazine .com/people-we-love-eco-me/).

Strategic Bootstrapping versus Reactionary Bootstrapping

As noted, bootstrapping is the most commonly used form of start-up financing, that is, using only insider finance. It is also known that most new businesses fail. There is a correlation between the two facts, and it is not co-incidence. Can entrepreneurs achieve any and all goals via bootstrapping? Certainly. Should they achieve their goals in this manner? Probably not.

The reason for this is that most bootstrappers are completely reactionary (Neely & Van Auken, 2012), and while flexibility and change are hallmarks of the start-up stage, there are certain knowable courses of action that can be taken. Reactionary techniques are those listed above as obvious, and they are generally undertaken when an entrepreneur cannot make ends meet for in any given period of time. Again, this is likely unavoidable, but these tactics should be kept to a minimum for they are unlikely to result in wealth creation. With the enormous amount of "unknowables" at this stage, when something can be known, it should be. Stated differently, research has shown that many activities can be taken in nascence and start-up to leverage bootstrapping to success—clearly these are knowables. These activities make up strategic bootstrapping and this book will shed light on them for the entrepreneur. It will offer a course of action that allows entrepreneurs to bootstrap their way to success—but only after considering all alternatives (e.g., requesting external funds).

The term *strategic bootstrapping* means deliberately bootstrapping with an overall goal of establishing a firm's competitive advantage, rather than just surviving another day. Ideally, a given firm can survive *and* establish a competitive advantage. In this way, the firm has a greater likelihood of exiting a resource constrained configuration and entering a configuration of relative bounty. When conceptualized this way, the positive aspects of bootstrapping can be distilled into a deliberate course of action. Of course, this deliberate plan will require constant tweaks and changes as the entrepreneur reacts to environmental forces. However, the main point here is that there is a way (in many contexts) to use only internal financing and still build wealth. And while this book does not necessarily endorse the general practice of bootstrapping, it does acquiesce that the majority of start-ups will bootstrap—for better or worse.

The Structure of the Book

Following this introductory chapter, Chapter 2 will discuss the key underpinnings of new firms. The idea here is that before we can consider financing issues, a broader, more fundamental understanding of why financing decisions are so important in new firms—and how these decisions differ remarkably from more mature firms. This will also set the stage for the new venture development model in Chapter 5.

Chapter 3 discusses bootstrapping from largely a financial viewpoint. In light of the fundamental challenges facing new firms—discussed in Chapter 2—we move to discussing financing and how these challenges affect financing decisions in new firms. This will be a relatively broad discussion, but it will give the reader some important paradigms that can then be used to make new firm financing decisions in numerous contexts. Bootstrapping really cannot be understood well without an understanding of new venture finance theory.

Chapter 4, then, looks at two main issues. First, why do entrepreneurs bootstrap? What is their motivation? It is important for entrepreneurs to understand that humans often have implicit biases that effect decision making, and entrepreneurs are certainly no exception. Second, this chapter will examine types of bootstrappers and types of bootstrapping. Some bootstrappers seem to do better than others and some forms of bootstrapping seem to work better than others.

Following this, Chapter 5 moves to more directly assisting the entrepreneur to understand how to bootstrap in a strategic fashion. After briefly reviewing some dominant theories, specific and actionable prescriptions are made. There is a strong focus on things entrepreneurs can do before starting their businesses.

Finally, Chapter 6, the theme of offering prescriptions is continued. However, in this chapter, ideal individual and organizational typologies are offered. Specifically, if entrepreneurs can engage in certain behaviors and form certain types of firms, they can greatly enhance their chances of profitably growing so that bootstrapping will no longer be a necessity.

CHAPTER 2

Bootstrapping and the Problem of Being New

About This Chapter

This chapter outlines the issues associated with newness. As noted, new ventures fail at a much higher rate than older firms and while this may seem commonsensical, there is value in understanding exactly why new firms are so apt to fail. If we can drill down into this failure rate, to identify specific aspects of newness, then we might be able to devise ways around them to increase our chances of success—even for bootstrappers.

For example, pundits will often report that the most common cause of new firm failure is "a lack of capital." While this is most certainly the case, the reasoning is circular and therefore not all that helpful to the entrepreneur. Eventually, every firm fails because of a lack of capital. If a given firm cannot perform value-added activities in a way that generates more cash than it spends, that firm will eventually fail. The more interesting questions are things like: why did a given firm not receive enough revenue from customers? Why did a given firm have such an elevated cost-structure? And, more germane to our current topic, why was a given firm unable or unwilling to receive external financing?

Take for example, Planet Popcorn, a new venture that produces and retails gourmet popcorn. A textbook example of bootstrapping and hustle, the business was started with a small amount of the owner's savings and leveraged with a loan from the owner's mother. This venture has revenue in excess of $2 million, and a high degree of legitimacy via a contract with Disney. By these key measures, the product is a good one—customers enjoy the popcorn. In spite of this, the firm cannot turn a profit and the entrepreneur is struggling to locate reasonable external financing. As a

result, the firm faces a relatively quick demise (http://www.theprofitfans
.com/2014/planet-popcorn-the-profit-cnbc-season-1-episode-3.html).
Clearly, the owner realizes that she has a lack of capital, but this explana-
tion does not provide her much in the way of assistance. She needs to
understand why, with solid revenue, her firm is not profitable and unable
to attract external financing.

To shed light on plights like Planet Popcorn's, we will introduce the
related concepts of legitimacy, signaling, and newness liabilities. The work
that experts have done exploring these concepts give us a deeper understanding of the "lack of capital" problem and ultimately an understanding
of why new firms—particularly bootstrapped firms—are prone to failure.

Before exploring the current thinking and evidence on these key issues, it is important to address the central figure in all of this—the entrepreneur. If entrepreneurs are not clear in articulating what they ultimately
desire from the new business, then they are likely in for some rough years
(Kuratko & Hodgetts, 2006). Specifically, the entrepreneur should consciously identify the values, beliefs, and norms that are important to
them. Then work to clearly understand how the business will be an exten-
sion and reinforcement of these things. This way, entrepreneurs can make
consistent decisions that will be a positive reflection of them (Rutherford,
Buller, & Stebbins, 2009).

Engage in Self-Reflection

Possibly the most important activity in which an entrepreneur can engage
before start-up is not very active at all. Time must be spent here deciding
what outcomes are desired from the venture. One way to conceptual-
ize this is by employing Noam Wasserman's dichotomy of "rich or king"
(Wasserman, Nazeeri, & Anderson, 2012). Wasserman submits that entrepreneurs must make a decision early on regarding whether they chiefly
desire to be king—that is, maintaining more or less complete ownership
in the business—or rich. The decision to be rich likely requires that the
entrepreneur take outside equity. The choice to become rich obviously
dilutes the entrepreneur's ownership stake and possibly will result in the
entrepreneur being removed as CEO at some point, but the choice to be
king likely constrains the entrepreneur and often results in stunted growth

and lower overall valuation in the future. The genesis of Wasserman's point can be summarized by the following statement: The king entrepreneur will likely end up with a much larger share of the pie, but the rich entrepreneur will likely end up with a smaller share of a much larger pie.

Ultimately, this must be a choice that reflects the values of the entrepreneur, but entrepreneurs must not fool themselves that they can be both king and entrepreneur. While achieving both happens (Wasserman offers up examples like Bill Gates with Microsoft, Anita Roddick with The Body Shop, and Phil Knight of Nike), these instances are outliers and not typical. The vast majority of entrepreneurs do not accomplish this goal. Most entrepreneurs that keep control do not reach high levels of growth or wealth creation, and most entrepreneurs that grow their firms substantially do not maintain a high level of control.

This choice will have many implications for how the entrepreneur would like to proceed, particularly with regard to choice of financing. Rich entrepreneurs need to understand that their "baby" will likely be taken away from them at some point. Also, they need to position themselves in nascence for a high level of top-line growth. Big-time equity players (i.e., venture capital firms) want market and revenue growth, and quickly. As noted, they want a relatively quick and very profitable exit. While containing costs and expenses is paramount for the king entrepreneur, the rich entrepreneur will have to worry a bit less about these issues and will need to focus more on driving revenue and quantity.

King entrepreneurs, on the other hand, will be reluctant to accept equity—especially early on. It bears repeating, though, that even if entrepreneurs decide that they do not want to sell a portion of the company, they may still consider outside debt. Moreover, angels and private investors will often take a minority stake in the business, thereby allowing the entrepreneur to increase resources bases without giving up total control. In addition, king entrepreneurs will have to be astute business people by constantly and creatively doing more with less and likely working very hard.

Time may be the most important asset of a bootstrapped entrepreneur. This is because of the simple fact that many, many things must get done in a bootstrapped start-up and there is little money to pay staff. If the entrepreneur does not possess the necessary time to perform these tasks himself, they will not get done. This is often termed *sweat equity*, which is another term that is often stated and seldom explained. It is the entrepreneur's time invested into the firm. Like actual equity, the entrepreneurs cannot invest what they do not have.

This rich versus king discussion highlights and reinforces this book's focus on a more causal or rational approach to starting a venture. Without the benefit of a more causal approach, valuable reflection may never take place, and this lack of reflection may result in a lot of undesired outcomes.

Newness

Moving to less personal concerns, as perspective entrepreneurs consider whether or not to bootstrap, it is important for them to be aware of the basic fundamental facts that underlie start-ups. Once these are understood, entrepreneurs can make more informed decisions before and after start-up that will assist them in financially and strategically structuring their new venture to survive and thrive.

Before any financial fundamentals are discussed, though, it makes sense to cover some more general notions of the start-up experience. Armed with these rudiments, we can then move to weighing the pros and cons of bootstrapping, and if bootstrapping is the preferred mode of operation we can discuss ideal tactics to help the entrepreneur flourish with relatively few resources.

It is little secret that most new ventures fail, however the reasons underlying that failure rate are numerous—virtually infinite. Fortunately, experts have organized these reasons for us so that we can understand them and hopefully avoid them. Unfortunately, though, many things known by experts are not effectively communicated to practicing entrepreneurs. Here, we will attempt to do exactly that.

First, new ventures fail simply because they are, well, new. This may seem obvious, but stick with me as we explore this innate newness and exactly what it means. As an analogy, consider a newborn baby and visualize all the inherent problems that a baby has surviving in the world. Physiologically, he has developed very few of the properties that a healthy, robust human needs. He cannot feed himself or protect himself. He is highly susceptible to disease—without his parents or caregivers he would perish. He needs help from the outside world and the more help he receives, the better his chances for survival and healthy growth.

Moreover, the more nurturing he received in the womb has important effects on his well-being after birth. Even if he has all of the support and nurturing that he needs, there is still the issue of time. It simply takes time for him to grow up—to develop the physiological and social skills that he needs. As he receives the support, protection, and nutrients that he needs, he grows. Fortunately, most newborns have people who consider it their primary goal to supply these things.

Clearly, the new venture's situation is not so dire, but the comparison may be a closer one than we think. Just by virtue of being new, the venture must develop the internal systems that it needs to function and this is difficult (Stinchcombe, 1965). For example, logistics (no matter how simple) must be developed. As materials, supplies, and people come into the organization, they must be managed effectively and efficiently. If the venture cannot add value to the inputs in an efficient manner, it will not survive long. Consider this the new firm's physiology.

External relationships with suppliers must be developed so that these items can come into the organization, and customer relationships must be developed to allow the firm to receive the primary nutrient it needs to survive—cash. Unlike the baby, though, the venture has no outsiders that consider it their primary job to supply this cash to firm. In fact, many of the outsiders are aggressively working to keep this cash from the new venture. Also unlike the baby, the new venture must proactively fight these competitors for the nutrients that it needs.

If the new venture were simply born into a world of other new ventures, there would far less of an issue. All ventures would have virtually the same deficiencies and the playing field would be somewhat level— babies competing against babies, if you will. This is not the case. By definition, most firms will be far more established than the new venture, and therefore will have some stock of cash, customers, suppliers, and general networks that it takes to thrive as a business. Moreover, just by virtue of *not* being new, the established ventures will have some degree of reputation, credibility, and legitimacy that will increase its chances of gaining further resources. Clearly, the new firm must start from scratch to develop these things that other competitors have already developed. This term, *from scratch*, becomes a central one when considering new ventures, as it attempts to capture the notion that the entrepreneur must make something from nothing in a relatively short period of time.

Consider for example, 1-800-Got-Junk. Brian Scudamore founded this company in 1989 in Vancouver with a $700 truck. While many of his competitors were not large or sophisticated, they were old and had established customer contacts and reputations. He understood, though, that customers would value a garbage removal system that was consistent, professional, and fair. Through hustle and frugal living, Brian was able to reinvest profits and eventually establish a franchise. He now has more than 200 franchises and the company has implemented a central call center for all stores, which serves to further his strategy of consistency in a fragmented, inconsistent industry. By simply displaying more reliability than his competitors, Scudamore was able to shed his newness relatively quickly by appearing old compared to other firms in the industry. However, like most well-known examples, 1-800-Got-Junk is an outlier.

Far more common is a company like Tidewater Landscaping (name changed). This firm was established in 2012 to provide upscale landscape architecture solutions to wealthy clients in the tidewater region of Virginia. Using a strategy similar to Brian Scudamore's, the firm was unable to steal away clients from the established landscapers in the area even though the service was of superior quality and professionalism. It simply is the case that, lacking some very clear value proposition, most consumers dislike new products/services. The company liquidated in 2013.

These examples illustrate what scholars often call the "liability of newness." The term is employed to capture the many factors that make up the fact that new ventures face a much higher mortality rate than older ventures. This liability is not a literal one—you will not find it on a balance sheet—but it is descriptive in capturing the notion that new firms, by definition, are disadvantaged in myriad ways simply because they are not old.

Virtually every new firm will face these liabilities and they are, collectively, the reason for the extremely high failure rates of new ventures (Stinchcombe, 1965). This begs the question: what can be done about being new? Can a venture start old? Literally, no, but once one understands two main issues, one can begin to shed these liabilities and ultimately be free of them as quickly as possible: (1) if stakeholders *perceive* the venture is old (or at least not new), that is almost as good as being old, and (2) time spent wisely in gestation can allow a firm to grow "in the womb" and be older at "birth." Obviously, entrepreneurs cannot effect the space/time continuum, therefore new ventures will always be new, but once we understand exactly what properties make stakeholders so hesitant to provide new ventures with resources, entrepreneurs can work to remove these properties—or least make them less apparent.

These liabilities are extremely important when considering whether or not to bootstrap, because generally overcoming them requires capital—exactly what the bootstrapper lacks. It will become clear, as we explore the reasons that external actors do not support new ventures, that many of these cannot be overcome without financial capital. However, as we will also explore, all is certainly not lost for the bootstrapper. A minority of bootstrappers craft strategies to survive and thrive, and we will explore these bootstrappers and their strategies. Importantly, we will also deeply explore the academic research—much of it empirical—on bootstrapping. Indeed, it is the goal of this work to provide the reader with as much evidence-based guidance in understanding and overcoming these liabilities as possible.

Overcoming Newness Liabilities

Possibly, the most appropriate way to explore overcoming newness liabilities is to consider the new venture's primary goal at start-up as—not a quest for tangible resources (e.g., cash)—but a quest for something far more subtle. That something is *appropriateness* in the eyes of important audiences or stakeholders. Appropriateness describes very well what the new venture lacks and what makes stakeholders hesitant.

For example, Airbnb is a privately-held online marketplace allowing anyone from private residents to commercial properties to rent out their extra space. Airbnb charges a 3 percent fee to those leasing out their space and a 6 to 12 percent fee to renters. Its growth in revenue is directly related to the site's growing popularity among travelers on a budget.

Now relatively well known, the firm began with a novel idea and passionate entrepreneurs, but people naturally fear change—or things that challenge their view of what is appropriate. The company had a great deal of trouble initially attracting customers and other resources. While the idea has some innate appeal, why would people rent rooms to strangers? Moreover, there were established competitors already in the space—not to mention hotels that may move aggressively to thwart the entrepreneurs. Humans have learned that inappropriate things—while periodically exciting—are often dangerous. Airbnb was eventually accepted into Paul Graham's Y Combinator program, but even Mr. Graham was skeptical of the idea from the start (http://blogs.wsj.com/venturecapital/2011/07/25/airbnb-from-y-combinator-to-112m-funding-in-three-years/). This example illustrates that even very high-quality new firms struggle to overcome newness liabilities.

When considering the importance of appearing appropriate, the question becomes what does appropriate look like in this context? This is pretty straightforward—appropriate looks like an old, large business. Clearly a new venture cannot be old and large, but fortunately, stakeholders (especially customers) do not often engage in due diligence to uncover every aspect of a new venture. They will look for only a few characteristics and if those check out, their concerns over inappropriateness, and therefore the venture's liabilities of newness fade away (Bitektine, 2011). Moreover, humans attempt to be efficient with their time and energy. They will only actively work to judge the things that they absolutely must. They are perfectly willing to defer to some expert or maven when making judgments about the appropriateness of a given venture (Rosch, 1978). They know that if certain informed people or institutions have judged a given firm as legitimate, then they are reasonably safe in also making that judgment. So, if the entrepreneur can garner support from a base of trusted individuals (or one individual like Paul Graham), that entrepreneur will find each subsequent individual easier to convince.

The Importance of Legitimacy in the New Venture

So, what are these specific things on which external actors make judgments? Not surprisingly, it depends. First, on type of audience: To whom does the venture want to appear appropriate? The answer is probably "all of them," but new ventures must prioritize stakeholders (Jawahar & McLaughlin, 2001). Early on, it is the cash grantors that must be courted because they have what new venture needs most. This does not mean that entrepreneurs will want to overtly dismiss other types of stakeholders, but they will want to be careful in how they allot their time.

Different stakeholders look for different things and use different judgment processes when considering appropriateness. Experts have distilled much of this knowledge into a concept known as legitimacy. Legitimacy is defined as ". . . a social judgment of acceptance, appropriateness, and desirability [that] enables organizations to access other resources needed to survive and grow" (Zimmerman & Zeitz, 2002). Again, this idea of appropriateness comes up. In many ways, the new venture simply does not want to arouse any suspicion. That is appearing to be just like every other established, successful organization. Simultaneously, though, the new venture will want to communicate its special features—its distinctiveness. This conundrum is critical when considering the problem of bootstrapping in the new venture.

So, the entrepreneur must clearly understand what stakeholders want to see in terms of similarity and what they want to see in terms of difference. As importantly, entrepreneurs should understand where a given audience wants to see these things. Customers for example, want to feel the firm and its products are useful and reliable (Hannan & Freeman, 1988), so entrepreneurs will certainly want to trumpet how their product meets the customer's needs. The entrepreneur will also want to do it in way that communicates permanence. The entrepreneur can also communicate difference here, so that the customer understands why it is better than competing products, but the entrepreneur will want to communicate this in appropriate ways. Further, the entrepreneur will want to give the impression that product or service is produced and delivered in a bona fide and reliable (i.e., nondifferent) way. Consider the advice from entrepreneur and venture capitalist, Guy Kawasaki: "You can innovate in technology, markets, and customers, but inventing a new business model is a bad bet" (Kawasaki, 2004). His point being that stakeholders want to see innovative products and services delivered in tried and true ways. New business models often signal inappropriateness.

Financiers on the other hand, want their invested capital back along with some rate of return. This group of stakeholders is far more calculative when judging appropriateness, but can be impacted by influential others. We will discuss financiers at length in the next chapter.

For the employee, the metrics researched will be fairly specific. This stakeholder will assess benefits offered, pay scale, and possibilities for advancement. Human resource structures may also come into play here (e.g., employee handbook, worker's compensation coverage, payroll direct deposits, paid time off [Govardhan &Williamson, 2000]). This is essentially an active search to judge whether or not the new firm lines up with other bona fide employers in these regards.

The Importance of Signaling in the New Venture

The things that the entrepreneur attempts to communicate to important audiences are collectively termed *signals* and an understanding of the nature of quality signals will greatly enhance the entrepreneur's efforts at attaining this initial legitimacy from stakeholders.

Because new firms have very little in the way of history, they must utilize more novel communication tactics than more mature firms. This process is central to new firm survival and directly informs the decision to bootstrap. Very briefly, signaling in the new firm context gets at the notion that, because these firms lack historical financial statements they must engage in things like pitching, image management, and puffery to communicate legitimacy to stakeholders. If they are able to do this effectively, they can attain positive judgments of legitimacy, receive resources, and outperform competitors. This notion will be discussed throughout the next few chapters.

As noted, different groups of stakeholders look for different things, but ultimately it comes back to appropriateness—and new is usually inappropriate. It should be noted that there are also multiple types of legitimacy that may be pursued, but that nuance is better left for another time. Again, the notion of appropriateness is what is most key. And what is most important here is that to signal appropriateness is very often expensive—clearly not good news for bootstrapping entrepreneur.

Summary

This chapter explains why firms fail and why this matters to the future or current bootstrapper. Hopefully, the reader can see that newness is the core overriding problem of the start-up and bootstrapping likely does little to counteract this problem and probably exacerbates it. But, now that we know the root of the problem we can begin to creatively find ways to "be older." Even for the bootstrapper, this is possible. It is just very difficult and therefore is virtually impossible to do if the entrepreneur is completely reactionary at start-up. Entrepreneurs must be deliberate in their tactics and behaviors if they are to overcome this daunting challenge—they must be strategic. These strategic recommendations aimed at bootstrappers will be developed fully in the upcoming chapters—specifically legitimacy and signaling. An understanding of these issues will then allow us to create a more specific roadmap for the bootstrapper in nascence and beyond.

Now that we understand the underlying cause of new venture failure, we spend the next chapter fully exploring the nature of financing in the new venture. Often neglected in the entrepreneur's education is an elucidation of finance principles specifically tailored for the new venture. The next chapter will serve as a primer on new venture finance.

CHAPTER 3

New Venture Finance Considerations for the Bootstrapper

About This Chapter

How a new firm is financed matters. Accordingly, Chapter 3 presents an overarching, if general, discussion of new venture finance. To more completely understand what may and may not work as a bootstrapper, we need to more fully understand some basic rudiments of capital structure in new firms. Chapter 2 covered the fact that new firms struggle to receive support from important stakeholders because those stakeholders believe that new firms, on average, are not legitimate vis-à -vis more mature firms. Through this discussion, the new venture fundamentals introduced in Chapter 2 are extended by examining and explaining how they impact capital structure in new firms. This will result in a primer on new venture finance, including options for funding.

While capital structure—generically defined as a firm's mix of debt and equity—is actively researched, the majority of studies have been conducted with mature firms in mind. The relative shortage of research into private new firm capital structure is troubling because these firms provide about half of private sector employment and produce about half of private sector output in the United States (Vinturella & Erickson, 2003). These entrepreneurs need evidenced-based guidance for making decisions around debt and equity. This chapter endeavors to provide exactly that by covering issues critical specifically to the new venture.

In covering new venture finance fundamentals, here we focus more specifically on one group of stakeholders—financiers. As noted, financiers often expect fairly specific outcomes from investments in new ventures and those outcomes are often objective and measurable financial metrics. This stands in contrast to customers, who generally want to be satisfied with the usefulness and reliability of a product or service.

For example, Argosy, a private equity firm, clearly states that its managers will only invest in firms with revenues in excess of $15 million and cash flow of $3 to $9 million, and will never invest in retail firms (http://www.argosyprivateequity.com/about-argosy/investment-criteria/). Other firms or individuals may be less strict in their requirements for investments, but most will still invest only when the present value of the future returns from the new venture is calculated and estimated to be greater than the proposed present value of the investment (Brealey & Myers, 1991).

Compare Argosy with Garage Technology Ventures. This venture capital (VC) firm is keenly focused on investing only "seed" or early stage financing. Even so, they also have exacting standards. They will invest in firms developing software, clean-tech, and material sciences—but never life sciences. Further, they will only invest in firms that require less than $5 million to break even (http://www.garage.com/about/).

Similar to the tone set in the last chapter, we drill down into the underlying reasons why lack of funding has such deleterious effect on the future of the firm. Not surprisingly, the reasons are related to the notions of newness liabilities, and the fact that overcoming these liabilities generally requires financial capital. Stated differently, to create a perception of age, money will likely need to be spent. For the bootstrapper, understanding these reasons is critical because, while research indicates that overcoming these challenges is difficult without external funding, it is possible. In addition, nascent entrepreneurs may realize that accepting this funding is not as onerous and restrictive as they believe.

The Funding Gap

New firms face very different financial markets compared to mature firms—particularly public firms. This difference is often captured by the so-called "funding gap." The funding gap describes the situation where there are many new venture entrepreneurs in the population, and most of them need funding. However, there are fewer providers of funding, and therefore many entrepreneurs cannot get access to funding. Thus, a gap exists.

Recall that Airbnb founders Brian Chesky and Joe Gebbia could not attract any funding for their start-up in 2007. To raise money, the two came up with the idea of selling novelty breakfast cereals like "Obama O's" and "Cap'n McCains," which actually generated more than $30,000 for the start-up. Two years later, they were still unable to attract funding when they were invited to join Y Combinator—a well-known business incubator and accelerator. In April 2009, the entrepreneurs finally landed $600,000 in funding from well-known VC firm, Sequoia Capital Markets (http://blogs.wsj.com/venturecapital/2011/07/25/airbnb-from-y-combinator-to-112m-funding-in-three-years/). This is a prime example of how difficult it can be for even apparently high quality new firms to attract funding.

Difficulties, such as these, exist because new firm owners face less organized, less informationally efficient, and therefore more restrictive financial markets (Berger & Udell, 1998). In other words, there is no established formal market for shares of new ventures. Since there is no market, seeking funding can be challenging and costly for the entrepreneur and financier—both in terms of time and money (Berger & Udell, 1998). Moreover, since there is also no share price for units of new ventures, terms of equity investments or "deals" are typically decided by negotiations between the entrepreneur and the investor (Rutherford, Coombes, & Mazzei, 2012). These are all marked disadvantages with regard to seeking and receiving external finance for the new firm.

Such a process creates a reality whereby prelegitimate ventures often perceive that they must rely only on seed financing from friends and family and high interest funding such as personal credit cards (Winborg & Landstrom, 2000). With all of these difficulties related to seeking funding, one might wonder what the advantages of receiving external finance are. Obviously, one answer would be *more money is better than less*, but clearly this is too simple, for if the firm has no plans for the money, it will likely be used inefficiently. Having too much cash on hand can result in a lack of discipline because entrepreneurs often feel compelled to spend invested money (Bhide, 1992). Because there is no slack, Amar Bhide likens bootstrapping to a just-in-time inventory system, whereby every expenditure (no matter how minor) is carefully scrutinized, and as a result, money is spent more wisely.

In short, the advantages of receiving external finance revolve around the finding that insufficient financing of new firms leads to lower levels of performance (Deeds, DeCarolis, & Chaganti, 1995). Sufficient capitalization at start-up, on the other hand, improves future prospects for growth (Alsos, Isaksen, & Ljunggren, 2006). This is the case because, over and above the money being received, the granting of finance by an external stakeholder often provides legitimacy. This granting sends a strong, honest signal to other participants (customers, suppliers, etc.) that some entity views the new venture as appropriate.

Accordingly, before discussing types of bootstrappers and the techniques that they may employ to creatively operate with minimal financing, it makes sense to discuss the different types of external financing options that exist. Therefore, below is an examination of broad sources of financing that might be available to the entrepreneur. Included in the discussion is an outlining of debt and equity choices that entrepreneurs may have at different stages of their firm's lives.

Types of External Financing

Elucidating funding types is key for a couple of reasons; first the stance of this book is that entrepreneurs should be preparing themselves to be in a position to receive more attractive forms of financing—even if they elect not to accept it at the outset. Second, research indicates that many entrepreneurs may not be aware of all the options available to them, and this often results in undercapitalization (Ebben, 2009).

Very broadly, there are two types of external financing that can be explored: debt and equity. In brief, debt describes a form of financing whereby the entrepreneur will not give up any ownership share, but must pay interest (in addition to principle) on the loan. Equity, on the other hand, requires no interest payment, but the entrepreneur is essentially selling a portion of the company to receive the capital and must share the profits and the proceeds if the firm is sold. It should be noted that there also exist a number of "hybrid" financing tools that investors employ. These tools combine features of both debt and equity to help both parties meet their needs. For example, convertible debt is relatively a commonly used vehicle that originates as debt, but can be converted to equity at a later date—usually after some additional money is raised by the new venture. Types of new venture financing are virtually limitless because they are ultimately the result of negotiations between financiers and entrepreneurs.

Debt Grantors

There is a broad range of financial institutions that provide debt to new ventures. While traditional banks are the most common, insurance companies, finance companies, savings companies, private individuals, credit unions, and even suppliers and customers can provide the firm with debt financing.

These institutions actually have many types of debt at their disposal— not just the standard term loan. From simple overdraft protection to lines-of-credit, financial institutions can provide critical capital to start-ups—for a fee (i.e., rate of interest), of course. Possibly the most important thing to keep in mind regarding debt grantors is that they realize that their best case scenario is a repayment of principal plus interest. This is a lucrative scenario, but not if the lender engages in risky loans. Almost by definition, a new venture is risky; therefore, lenders generally require personal guarantees (e.g., second mortgages, pledges of equipment, etc.) on behalf of the entrepreneur before they will loan money to a new venture.

Take for example David MacNeil, Founder of WeatherTech, a firm that manufactures luxury car mats. Though MacNeil had long been a successful salesman and vice president for a top automotive outfit, he was still forced to offer a second mortgage on his home to borrow $50,000 to launch his firm (http://forbesindia.com/article/cross-border/unlikely-luxury-$150-floor-mats-for-cars/38046/1).

As a note and exception, while government programs (e.g., Small Business Administration) can assist new ventures in raising money, the government seldom actually loans money directly to ventures. Instead, they will often work with private banks by offering a "guarantee" to the bank. In this agreement, the agency will approve the entrepreneur and the bank will loan the money. The agency, then, agrees to cover a large percentage of the balance if the entrepreneur defaults. This guarantee makes lenders more willing to lend than they would otherwise be.

Equity Grantors

Over $40 billion is awarded each year to entrepreneurs in the United States by equity financiers, including angel investors and venture capitalists (Angel Capital Association, 2012; National Venture Capital Association, 2012). This category could also be termed private equity, as virtually all equity invested in new ventures is private, that is—not public. However, the term *private equity* is generally reserved for professionally run, financially endowed firms that invest in later stage firms with the goal of selling that firm in the relatively near term. As noted, while public companies may sell shares on an exchange, there is no widely accessible formal market for shares of new ventures.

- Venture capitalists. These investors are generally highly sophisticated and highly capitalized. On average, VC firms will invest heavily (VC's invested $27 billion in 3,143 firms in 2012 [National Venture Capital Association Yearbook, 2014]) and demand a great deal of ownership. Like most equity investors, they invest with the intent of exiting so that they can get their investment and return back—either via an initial public offering or a sale to a strategic partner (e.g., a large competitor) (Puri & Zarutskie, 2012).
  For example, one renowned VC firm insists on majority ownership before they will invest in a new venture (Wasserman, 2008). While this may not be the norm, it is illustrative of the fact that the goal for most VC firms is to exercise substantial ownership control over any firm in which they invest. By attaining this control, they allow themselves to dictate terms of exit (e.g., share price, timing, buyer) and, of course, maximizing their return.
  Because of their laserlike focus on lucrative exits—and occasionally little else—VC's are sometimes maligned as "vulture capitalists." However, they often bring more to the

deal than money. The partners of VC firms often have large networks of valuable human and social capital, and they themselves are usually extremely knowledgeable in matters of running a new venture.

These firms are heavily discussed in the academic and popular press, but the number of new ventures that are financed by VC's is tiny. In fact, many researchers believe the number is less than 1 percent of all new firms (Puri & Zarutskie, 2012).

- Angels/Angel groups. These are relatively sophisticated individuals and groups who are generally less formal and less capitalized than VC's. In 2013, angels invested $25 billion in nearly 71,000 firms (http://www.angelcapitalassociation. org/aca-public-policy-protect-angel-funding/). However, they are more likely to invest in new ventures than venture capitalists.

  These individuals and groups are generally wealthy people who have an interest in investing in new ventures. Many times these individuals will be former or current entrepreneurs who have been successful and want to help other entrepreneurs while enjoying a return on their investment. Angels have many similarities with VC's, but they are more numerous and generally more accessible than their larger counterparts. These entities are also more likely to be local and may be more patient. An excellent resource for finding angels is the Angel List (https://angel.co/). Angel list is a portal that connects promising start-ups to a network of early-stage investors.

- Corporate Investors. While less celebrated than traditional venture capitalists, corporations often invest in new ventures and they are likely sitting on more cash presently than the VC community (Pozin, 2014). For example, Fuhu, the maker of android-based tablets for kids raised $55 million from large corporations, Acer and DreamWorks (http://www.forbes. com/pictures/elld45efeih/fuhu/). Well-known start-up, Uber raised millions of dollars from Google's consulting arm— Google Ventures.

- Crowdfunding. This entirely new form of financing is rapidly emerging. Crowdfunding involves a new venture attracting investors from "the crowd," usually on an internet platform. Here, the "the crowd" refers to those individuals who are not private investors, angels, or VC's, but would like to support a given venture or project financially. This form of financing is a substantial departure from traditional equity financing because equity investments from nonfamily, nonfriends is highly regulated. For example, to qualify as a private investor, an individual must have a net worth, or joint net worth with the person's spouse, that exceeds $1 million (excluding the value of the primary residence), or have an income exceeding $200,000 in each of the two most recent years or joint income with a spouse exceeding $300,000 for those years (U.S. Securities and Exchange Commission, n.d.). Oculus Rift, the inventers of a virtual reality headset, raised $2.4 million from almost 10,000 individuals using Kickstarter. With this capital infusion, the founders were able to develop a prototype. This prototype showed so much promise that the company was acquired by Facebook for $2 billion (http://www.forbes.com/sites/ chancebarnett/2014/05/01/2-billion-facebook-acquisition- raises-question-is-equity-crowdfunding-better/). Crowdfunding is generally broken down into four subsets. Rewards-based crowdfunding, in which an individual will donate money to a firm or project and receive a perk (e.g., t-shirt, mug, or prototype); lending-based crowdfunding, where an individual lends money to a project and expects to be repaid with interest; simple donation crowdfunding is a scenario where an individual will give money to a cause, band, or firm and expect nothing in return; equity-based crowdfunding is where the investor is seeking a return on any money invested. Websites like Kickstarter and Prosper have democratized the process of raising equity via the crowd. Theoretically, anyone can invest in any new venture via crowdfunding platforms.

However, this is currently not a reality because, though the Jumpstart Our Business Start-ups (JOBS) Act was signed into law in April 2012, and contains guidelines (in Title III) for small and new firms to raise money from nonaccredited investors (i.e., the crowd), the U.S. Securities and Exchange Commission (SEC) has yet to approve these guidelines. The SEC was to have these in place by December 2012, but at the time of this writing, this has not occurred.

Currently, rewards-based crowdfunding is the most popular, but this may change as the federal and state governments clear the way for equity-based crowdfunding. In the U.S., nonaccredited investors (i.e., the crowd) have never been able to take equity stakes in private enterprises, and it is believed that there is tremendous pent up demand for investing of this type (Juetten, 2014).

Now that we have a general understanding of financial providers for new ventures, we turn our attention to understanding why it is so difficult to attract funding from these providers.

The Bermuda Triangle

When considering the challenges associated with receiving outside funding, three important and intertwined concepts must be understood. This will assist the nascent entrepreneur in thinking through financing options—or lack thereof. These concepts are information asymmetry, moral hazard, and adverse selection.

Information Asymmetry. Information asymmetry is perhaps the most heavily investigated area in new firm capital structures. It is simply the term used to describe the basic condition that financiers have difficulty gathering information on the new firm. In contrast to publically traded firms—or even older small, private firms—where information exists in the form of financial statements, media reports, employment records, etc., there is limited data on new firms. This makes it very difficult to judge the quality of such a venture—at least for the outsider. The entrepreneur, on the other hand, has complete information on the new firm.

Hence, because one party is far more informed than the other, information about the firm is not symmetrical.

To further clarify, in a market where financiers cannot accurately gauge the quality of the product that they are buying, it is likely that the marketplace will contain generally poor-quality offerings—"lemons" (Akerlof, 1970). Uncertainty, then, exists as to the overall quality of the product or service being provided; this uncertainty can greatly influence the final decision to invest. As such, if the option is given to invest in an established, legitimate source—versus a source, such as a new venture, that lacks legitimacy—the legitimate firm will be the organization of choice, all things equal. Therefore, to shed its image as a potential lemon (based on uncertainty) and to obtain more desirable sources of financing, the new firm must enhance legitimacy by providing valuable and honest signals to financiers.

This was clearly the case with Airbnb, mentioned above. The founders of this start-up, in spite of having a viable idea and a lot of hustle, were simply unable to coax any investment from the banking or equity communities. To become a viable option to these entities they had to improvise, and through improvising, they persevered. This perseverance eventually signaled to financiers that the idea had merit and that the founders were competent. As such, these signals garnered them the legitimacy needed to receive investment. As stated by Scott Shane, "Simply surviving for a few years improves the odds that a new business will get money from external sources" (Shane, 2008).

Moral Hazard. Because the entrepreneur possesses information that the financier does not, the possibility exists that the entrepreneur will act in ways that maximize his own well-being to the detriment of the financier. Because the firm has little transparency, the financier may not be able to observe malfeasance and would suffer accordingly. This condition is termed moral hazard, and is caused largely because of the aforementioned asymmetrical information. Many stakeholders may struggle to identify moral hazard behavior, due to information asymmetry with regard to the new venture's operations and market offering (Shane & Venkataraman 2000).

In 2013, entrepreneur Claudio Osorio was convicted of misleading investors and misappropriating investor funds for his own use. Osorio owned a manufacturing firm, Innovida, which was launched to build low-cost housing in developing nations. After raising over $40 million from approximately 10 investors, Osorio moved the money to an off-shore account and used it to finance his own lavish lifestyle (http://www .miamiherald.com/2013/09/17/3632865/miami-businessman-claudio-osorio.html). While this activity is certainly not the norm, it is clearly very concerning to investors and encourages them to be very cautious when investing in new firms.

Adverse Selection. Finally, adverse selection is simply the likely outcome for new ventures because of moral hazard. Firms that are not transparent are unlikely to be selected by financiers. Even if they are selected, financiers are likely to "punish" them with a much higher price on the granted capital (e.g., higher interest rates or a larger percentage of ownership).

An important note about the academic literature: experts in the realm of new firm finance embrace the well-known Modigliani & Miller theory (Modigliani & Miller, 1958), as underpinning capital structure decisions made by firms—with important caveats. Briefly, this theory holds that in "friction-less" (i.e., no transaction costs or taxes exist) environments, modifying an entrepreneur's financing choices (i.e., capital structure) will not change that firm's value or the owners' wealth. Changing a companies' capital structure simply alters ways in which streams of net operating cash flow is divided between different classes of investors. In short, the type of financing that a firm attains has no effect upon the owners' wealth.

While this Nobel Prize–winning contribution has provided the bases for theory development to a generation of scholars, many in the arena essentially conclude that Modigliani and Miller's work is simply not as applicable in the new firm context. The primary reason being that their work assumes, among other things, that no transaction costs exist and that investors and managers have the same information about the firm. These assumptions are often violated when considering new firms. For example, while markets can readily gather information about existing firms, it is more difficult to assess the value (and the intentions) of a new firm—thereby greatly increasing transaction costs.

This is important because, again, it highlights that new firms are different and the lessons learned in mature firm environments may not be applicable to entrepreneurs. Specifically, here, information asymmetries are pervasive. Since Modigliani and Miller's (1958) seminal work, a large body of literature has evolved in search of explanations for companies' capital structure choices outside Modigliani and Miller's perfect capital markets. Those choices, which often result in bootstrapping, will be explored in the next chapter.

The Financial Growth Cycle

All of these forces, working together, form a sort of universal model for venture financing. Figure 3.1 depicts a sort of financial growth cycle (FGC). The FGC describes a condition where the financial needs and financing options change as an organization becomes larger, older, and less informationally opaque. The FGC suggests that firms lie on a size–age–information continuum where the smaller–younger–more opaque firms must bootstrap. The FGC predicts that as the firm grows, it becomes a more desirable firm and will gain access to, among other things, VC and bank loans. In the final stage of the growth paradigm, as the firm grows and becomes even more attractive, it is more likely to gain increased access to public equity (PE), long-term debt financing (LTD), or other more desirable options (Berger & Udell, 1998). Several empirical

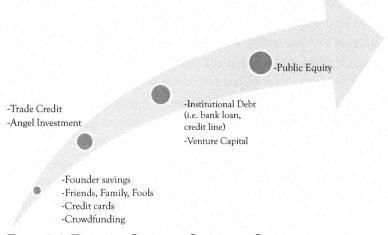

Figure 3.1 Financing Options as Legitimacy Grows

studies (Gregory et al., 2005) have found support for the notion that most new ventures emerge through the FGC as they grow and develop. Those which do not emerge through this cycle of financing ostensibly exit—they are failures.

It can be seen in Figure 3.1 that the sources of new firm financing differ significantly from those of large, publicly traded firms. On the debt side for new ventures, banks dominate. Equity for new businesses often initially comes from the entrepreneur, and in later stages, from angel investors and VC firms. However, it is important to keep in mind that most firms raise no outside money. Most firms bootstrap.

While the difference in institutions of choice between large and small businesses can be seen as a response to the information asymmetry and the entrepreneur characteristics discussed above, the institutional differences themselves could also cause capital structures of small firms to deviate from those of their larger counterparts.

Our present interest lies at the extreme left end of the FGC. Specifically, it is the purpose of this book to assist the entrepreneur in reaching the point where a young firm attains this "second level" of financing—moving away from vehicles such as personal credit cards and debt/equity from family and friends and instead toward institutional loans, trade credit, and angel or VC equity.

Summary

Research indicates that many entrepreneurs simply do not clearly understand the new venture financing process or all of the options available to them. The popular press unfortunately serves to exacerbate this problem by inordinately covering issues related to VC and other big money deals. This chapter set out to provide the reader with an overview of new venture finance with the hope of providing a more accurate picture.

So, one goal here was to give the reader a primer on new venture finance. Another goal of this book, though, is to give the entrepreneur tools to evaluate the decision of whether or not to accept financing. In the chapters following, we are primarily concerned with helping entrepreneurs to bootstrap their way to success, but it is extremely important that the entrepreneur thinks very carefully through the decision before launch.

Here, we attempted to provide the entrepreneur with tools needed to engage intelligently in this evaluation.

While classical models suggest that how a firm is financed is not a determinant of success, more recent research suggests that in new firms this is likely not the case. How a start-up is financed matters. Importantly, the amount of financing also matters, as this a key way that a firm can overcome newness liabilities.

CHAPTER 4

Financial Bootstrapping

About This Chapter

This chapter clarifies cutting edge thinking with regard to typologies of bootstrapping and bootstrappers. The field has developed generally—if not unanimously—agreed upon typologies of both. That is, not only are there differing motivations for avoiding external finance, there are also different types of bootstrapping tactics that one may use after the decision to bootstrap has been made, and importantly, these may lead to different outcomes. This is important because a chief goal of this book is to outline a path to financial success for the bootstrapper.

Chapter 3 laid down the underlying fundamentals of financing the start-up, and made a case for seeking external finance. This current chapter turns attention away from the financier to the entrepreneur with the hope that the reader will gain greater understanding into the underlying decision processes that affect entrepreneurs' desire to bootstrap. These cognitions impact their ability to bootstrap effectively.

Cognitions are also important because many entrepreneurs—like most humans—are unaware of their implicit biases. These biases are an interesting component of bootstrapping and entrepreneurship in general, because they are likely the driving factor behind an individual's decision to take up entrepreneurship as a career, which is certainly a good thing, however, these biases can also hamstring the entrepreneur by affecting key decisions in negative ways—particularly when it comes to relinquishing control. The tone remains that external finance can be very helpful for the new firm, but it is also understood that bootstrapping will likely be the modus operandi for most new venture entrepreneurs.

How Common Is Bootstrapping?

Bootstrapping is very common. Based on data from the Kauffman Firm Survey, only about 5 percent of start-ups use any source of external equity. This is equity from angels, venture capital (VC), or the government, and does not include equity from the entrepreneurs themselves or family members. However, approximately 20 percent of owners took on start-up debt in the form of a bank loan (personal or business) (Robb & Farhat, 2013). Even if it assumed that there is no overlap between the carriers of debt and equity, this still leaves approximately 75 percent of start-ups which used virtually no external finance. In addition, even those that used some form of external finance likely engaged in at least limited forms of bootstrapping—described below.

Therefore, regardless of motivation, the fact is that most new venture entrepreneur's bootstrap, and bootstrapping is part and parcel to the entrepreneurial experience. While this book stresses the importance of an entrepreneur's conscious decision to bootstrap, it also embraces the fact that many will still choose, or be forced to choose, this form of financing. As a result, it is critical that those considering new ventures verse themselves in the fundamental underpinnings so that they can survive and thrive in this challenging situation.

Why Do Entrepreneurs Bootstrap?

This is an interesting, and somewhat contentious, question that essentially comes down to one of two answers. The first is they have to. The second is they want to. There is compelling rationale for both answers and below we a take a deeper dive into each.

They Have to

This is the general assumption of many observers—that new firm founders would like to attract funding, but there simply are very few options available to these entrepreneurs (the aforementioned funding gap). Again, the funding gap describes a situation where there are many new venture entrepreneurs in the environment, and most are seeking funding. However, there are fewer willing providers of funding; therefore, many entrepreneurs cannot get access to funding. There is certainly some truth with regard to this situation. In general, funding options are far more limited for new firms than for older firms and the newer the firm, the fewer options available. In fact, the funding gap is often cited as the root of new firm failure (Blanchflower & Oswald, 1990).

Explanations for this condition generally revolve around resource dependence. That is, entrepreneurs are dependent upon resources from the environment and often cannot attain them. Therefore, they must find creative ways to "make due" with a lack of resources—bootstrapping.

Recall also that a number of studies find that due to market realities such as information asymmetry and uncertainties due to newness, financiers who do provide funding to new firms must essentially price such concerns into the costs charged for the financing (Ebben & Johnson, 2006). This higher price generally comes in the form of elevated interest rates or substantial dilution of the owner's stake.

This leads us to an important financial theory—that of static trade-off. Some researchers hold that entrepreneurs behave rationally, like managers of larger firms, and tend to target an ideal equity/debt mix. This, so-called *static trade-off theory*, explains entrepreneurs' choices for financing as a desire for profit and wealth maximization. The static trade-off theory departs from Modigliani and Meyer by suggesting that firms choose their capital structures by balancing the advantages of debt that are, for most part, tax related, and the disadvantages of debt, which arise mainly from the cost of financial distress and agency costs of debt (Masulis, 1980). In other words, entrepreneurs realize that markets are not without friction (e.g., taxes and agency costs). Because they realize this, they will very deliberately choose some ideal mix of debt and equity that maximizes profitability and/or cash flow.

Under this theory, the "Bermuda Triangle" often creates a "rock and hard place" dilemma for new venture entrepreneurs, even if they have founded a venture worthy of substantial investment. That is, they are seeking an optimal mix of external equity, but must choose to accept extremely costly debt or become overly diluted through accepting an onerous private equity offering. Under these two bad scenarios, entrepreneurs are likely to choose the least onerous and least expensive—inside equity (i.e., bootstrapping).

It is important to point out here that if the venture is able to survive and grow, many of these onerous terms dissolve. The entrepreneur can then target an ideal mix and raise this money with reasonable terms, much like other mature firms. Therefore, even if this path is not ideal for start-ups, slightly older ventures may perform very well by pursing a static trade-off plan.

They Want to

This is probably a less intuitive answer to why entrepreneurs bootstrap, but research tells us that it may be the right one. In fact, the main reason that entrepreneurs do not receive external financing is that they do not ask for it. They do not ask because they do not want it. They do not want it, because they want something else even more—autonomy (Shane, 2008). Decades of research indicates that a—if not *the*—reason that individuals pursue entrepreneurship is because they want to be their own bosses and they perceive that accepting external funds threatens this autonomy (Hessels, Van Gelderen, & Thurik, , 2008).

Consider the example of Zeynep Young who founded Double Line Partners to solve what she perceived to be a major problem in K-12 education. Double Line created a dashboard product that brings to educators a student's records for attendance, discipline, grades, credits, local benchmarks, state assessments, AP, ACT, and SAT scores (Lorek, 2014). Young wanted to make money with this venture, but she also wanted to follow her own path by focusing on the social good that the product could do. Realizing that equity investors primarily focus on maximizing revenue, she elected to bootstrap.

Work by finance scholars sheds some light on this condition as well. There exists a theory in the literature that is termed *pecking order theory.* This theory states that entrepreneurs have strong preferences regarding choice of financing and these choices are largely based on the entrepreneur's desire for autonomy (Winborg, 2009)—and not so much on a desire for wealth or revenue maximization. That is, on average, entrepreneurs prefer self-financing first, then external debt, and as a last resort, external equity. Once internal sources are exhausted, the preferred choice is to apply for a bank loan from a bank with which the firm has an existing banking relationship. Only after these options have been fully explored will an entrepreneur consider outside equity.

This school of thought maintains that the entrepreneur's characteristics and goals play a more important role than targeting some optimal debt–equity mix. In newer firms, entrepreneurs control the majority stake in the firm and often prefer to retain that control (Scherr & Hulburt, 2001). While the individual characteristics of entrepreneurs are not fully understood, it is important to understand that "ulterior" motives likely exist for entrepreneurs making the financing decisions. That is, motives other than profit—or even wealth—maximization. Stated differently, entrepreneurs will pay for autonomy—often large sums. Research indicates that entrepreneurs actually make 18 percent less than they would working for someone else (Kawaguchi, 2008). Ostensibly, because they value autonomy at least that much.

Though both motivations will likely still lead to bootstrapping, these two capital structure theories offer somewhat conflicting predictions on entrepreneurs' ideal choice of a financing vehicle. The static trade-off theory assumes that a certain optimal target capital structure exists for a firm and that, whenever investment opportunities arise, the firm acquires new financing in proportions suggested by that target capital structure. The pecking order theory holds that as long as entrepreneurs can minimally meet their needs with internal equity, they will. Only when they cannot will they consider outside debt or equity.

While both have received support in empirical studies of larger firms, in newer and smaller firms, the preponderance of data indicate that pecking order theory is better able to explain the choices of start-up entrepreneurs (Korkeamaki & Rutherford, 2006). Stated differently, entrepreneurs often make these important decisions based more upon their goals, preferences, and relationships rather than on a desire for wealth maximization. However, this does not mean that this is how they *should* make decisions.

Regardless, this leads to an interesting perspective—contrary to the view where entrepreneurs are forced to bootstrap based on a lack of resources, recent research suggests that bootstrapping may actually be a proactive and conscious strategy by the entrepreneur to lower costs and perceived risk (Carter & Van Auken, 2005; Grichnik & Singh, 2010;

Winborg, 2009) and to maintain control over decision making (Patel, Fiet, & Sohl, 2007), regardless of available capital. This feeds the debate as to whether or not bootstrapping might be more than a desperate option and, instead, may be deliberately chosen in order to provide the entrepreneur with certain advantages. This also feeds the debate of whether or not a true funding gap exists.

In attempting to solve the debate, researchers have investigated the motivations behind bootstrapping empirically. This research has led to a taxonomy of bootstrappers that specifically separates bootstrapping entrepreneurs into groups based upon primary motivation for eschewing external finance.

Types of Bootstrappers

This section outlines the research mentioned above. Indeed, findings indicate that various bootstrapping techniques are implemented based on the particular motivations of the founder (Winborg, 2009), and these motivations vary. Specifically, research indicates that there are at least three types of bootstrappers: cost-reducing, capital constrained, and risk reducing (Winborg, 2009). It is important to note that, even if entrepreneurs do consciously choose to bootstrap, they often do not make fully informed, rational decisions (Forbes, 2005). A summary of this typology is provided below in Table 4.1.

(1) Cost-reducing bootstrapper. This type of bootstrapper "wants to," and is driven by the desire to keep expenses and costs as low as possible. In addition to craving autonomy, these entrepreneurs ostensibly dislike the notion that debt comes with an interest expense and the process of requesting and receiving equity investment is also

Table 4.1 Summary of bootstrapper typologies

Bootstrapper type	Motivation	Dominant techniques used
Cost-reducing	Wants to	Share space, barter, borrow
Capital-constrained	Has to	Pay bills late, use founder's credit cards, forego salary
Risk-reducing	Wants to	Lease instead of buy, hire temporary workers, use Just-in-Time inventory system

expensive. There is the very real expenditure of time and money that accompanies raising money. That is especially salient for those entrepreneurs attempting to raise equity, as this can be a full-time job in itself.

Goldstar is the world's largest online seller of discounted concerts tickets. Started by three young entrepreneurs with $1,000, they purposely avoided outside investment because they felt that it resulted in inefficiencies and represented little upside (http://www.softwarebyrob.com/2011/09/01/ten-highly-successful-bootstrapped-startups/). The founders had previously worked for a VC-backed new venture that did not attract customers and failed. They felt strongly that the invested capital encouraged employees to be less frugal and that resulted in waste (Linderman, 2011). By streamlining operations and spending time coding and designing, rather than raising money, Goldstar has grown rapidly, selling approximately $40 million in tickets in 2011.

(2) Capital-constrained bootstrapper. This group of bootstrappers "has to" and is motivated by the simple fact that financing is not available for them and their businesses. These entrepreneurs either requested capital and were denied or perceived that such a request would be useless. Therefore, to realize their dream of business ownership they must operate as cheaply and creatively as possible.

This was the case with the popular online music service, Pandora. Though the new firm attracted seed funding at founding, that money evaporated quickly and the firm simply could not attract any debt or equity. As a result, the founders asked its remaining 50 employees to work for free for two and half years—paying them in stock options that might never be redeemable. Founder Tim Westergreen reported that he even considered gambling to raise money for the struggling start-up (Shinal, 2011). For Pandora, this was effective. They are now a public company and the number one online music service.

(3) Risk-reducing entrepreneurs. These folks also "want to," and are driven by the need to limit downside risk by eschewing investment, thereby keeping such investment off of the balance sheet. The apparent idea being: "if you do not receive external money, then you cannot lose external money." These entrepreneurs are similar to the

cost-reducing entrepreneurs, but ultimately are driven by the desire start small and exit cheaply and quickly, if necessary.

Types of Bootstrapping

A well-developed stream of research also exists with regard to the specific tactics that entrepreneurs use to survive during bootstrapping. While typologies abound, some consensus seems to have been reached around the three broad categories: cash cycle exploitation, minimizing investment, and joint utilization.

(1) Cash cycle exploitation. This first tactic is delaying payments and/ or minimizing receivables so that the entrepreneur may simply hang on to cash longer. This is a very simple technique and simply involves expediting the cash cycle in the entrepreneur's favor. That is, the entrepreneur understands that the key metric at start-up is cash flow. Regardless of how good the income statement looks, if entrepreneurs are not collecting their receivables, failure is imminent.

At least in the short run, if entrepreneurs can collect receivables very quickly and pay bills very slowly, they can effectively create a positive cash flow. Clearly, there are trust and relationship issues to consider here between entrepreneurs and their stakeholders, but these issues may be less pressing than survival.

(2) Minimize investment. This group of techniques also addresses the genesis of bootstrapping. Because one must rely on only the resources at hand, frugality becomes paramount. While effectively minimizing investments and expenses is always a goal of a firm, bootstrapped new ventures are in an extreme situation.

Techniques in this category include leasing equipment, living in the office, understaffing, foregoing attorneys and accountants by using software, etc. This describes entrepreneur Greg Gianforte well. While he did eventually accept a large amount of equity, he started Right-Now—a software solution that helps firms handle large amounts of email—from his house and did not hire any employees until he was generating revenues of $30,000 per month (http://www.inc.com/magazine/20020201/23855.html). Even when he was able to hire sales people and move to a larger location, he chose an abandoned elementary school to keep overhead as low as possible.

(3) Joint utilization. Our final category is sometimes termed relationship-oriented bootstrapping, and it involves working with other institutions (possibly even competitors) to share resources. Examples here include sharing employees, equipment, office space, utilizing trade credit, and bartering with others.

Possibly the most fruitful version of this involves partnering with customers in ways that encourage them to cover part or all of a product or services development costs up front. This is what Michael Brill did when he started Crushpad, a San Francisco-based firm that connects wine enthusiasts with his wine-making facility. This connection allows customers to order the grapes and have them delivered to Crushpad. The customers then arrive at Crushpad and use Brill's equipment to make their own wine (Quackenbush, 2010). While Brill must maintain the equipment and pay other overhead, his customers pay up front for any other supplies.

Summary

Entrepreneurs who make the decision to bootstrap (or who have no choice but to bootstrap) are left to their own creative devices with little or no assistance from external funding sources. And it is the case that most start-ups bootstrap, whether "they want to" or "they have to."

Accordingly, bootstrapping becomes a necessity in order for the entrepreneur to overcome resource constraints, and to optimize the resources that are accessible. The entrepreneur is compelled to generate alternative solutions that are superior to those developed in situations where capital is readily available (Grichnik & Singh, 2011). They must contend with various liabilities (e.g., financing, legitimacy, inexperience), and determine the most parsimonious ways in which to overcome them. In contending with these liabilities, it is hoped the entrepreneur will consider the full range of bootstrapping options and not simply rely on the most obvious (i.e., cash cycle exploitation).

In nascence, it is hoped that entrepreneurs will fully consider their options before deciding to forego external funding. It is also hoped that the reader will take some time in nascence to consider their motivation for bootstrapping. It is likely that entrepreneurs who "want to" face better odds (Carpentier & Suret, 2006). To put a fine point on it, if they have been denied funding or cannot attract funding, it may be that the venture is simply not viable. Nascence is a very cheap time for the entrepreneur to realize this, and this is also an ideal time to pivot.

This chapter endeavored to assist the entrepreneurs in understanding why they may have a desire to bootstrap—and that desire may not be entirely rational. However, it also laid out broad tactics for bootstrapping and hopefully communicated that not all tactics are equal. More detailed tactics will be presented in Chapter 5, but they will build specifically on the typologies and taxonomies presented here.

CHAPTER 5

Bootstrap Strategically

About This Chapter

This chapter departs from the previous four chapters by focusing more on the *strategic* aspect of strategic bootstrapping. That is, here, we offer more specific advice to the entrepreneur based on the preceding chapters.

As noted, bootstrapping is made up of two general components: (1) the decision to avoid external finance, and (2) the creative techniques used to operate in a situation with little capital. Having discussed the first of these components in some detail, this chapter will look prescriptively at the second component of bootstrapping. That is, once the decision has been made to start without this financing, what creative tactics should be employed to operate in this resource-constrained environment?

To begin, let us reconsider a basic question: what do new firms need to thrive? They need resources from stakeholders. Is bootstrapping likely to yield those resources? It is fairly evident that, on average, forgoing external resources in nascence or at start-up will not yield resources—by definition. The primary thrust of this book is to report that research indicates that those bootstrappers generally struggle to grow and build wealth. Theory suggests it and evidence supports it. While not a unanimous opinion of scholars, at present, the theoretical and empirical evidences seem to support this relation.

Indeed, the research reviewed in this book is highly suggestive of a negative relationship between bootstrapping and performance—at least performance as defined as revenue growth, employment, and wealth creation. Bootstrapping may have a slight positive relationship with survival (Rutherford, Coombes, & Mazzei, 2012). This is no trivial thing, but entrepreneurs must be careful in satisficing with simple survival. There is evidence that many entrepreneurs who cannot "cash out" in some way are destined to make less than they would working for someone else, while working longer hours (Moskowitz & Jorgensen, 2002). And, it would appear that firms that bootstrap at start-up are less likely to be able to cash out.

Now, this may be acceptable to many entrepreneurs, as additional research indicates that surviving entrepreneurs of all profiles are happier than others (Kawaguchi, 2002). However, and this important, what if there were a method whereby entrepreneurs could be *both happy and wealth creating*, for research also indicates that happiness is strongly and positively correlated with wealth. Outlining that method is the goal of this chapter, but the entrepreneur should understand that the bootstrapped road is a tough one. Therefore we now assume that, for better or worse, the entrepreneur has either tried to attain funding and failed or has decided not to attempt it—and still wishes to start a business.

A General Model of New Venture Survival and Growth

The strategic aspect focuses more on the customer than the financier, because our key outcome here is revenue—not funding. So, we now leave the financier stakeholder and more squarely focus on the customer. There is an essential, if simple, distinction that often gets lost in the rhetoric: while startups can often benefit from funding, if a business is not selling products or services to customers, that entrepreneur does not technically have a business. Also, important there is the fact that sending signals to customers is different than sending signals to financiers.

How can resource constrained entrepreneurs send signals to attract legitimacy from customers? To answer this question, we introduce a somewhat generic model of new venture development shown in Figure 5.1 that will allow us to make more pointed advice throughout the chapter.

Fortunately, research has uncovered a number of ways that a bootstrapper could be successful in sending high-quality signals to customers. However, to do this requires that the entrepreneur engage in some deliberate strategizing. That is, the entrepreneur cannot do what most bootstrappers do by simply allowing strategic direction to emerge. As Henry Mintzberg states, ". . . strategy formation walks on two feet, one deliberate, the other emergent" (Mintzberg & Waters, 1985).

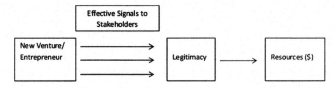

Figure 5.1 A general model of new venture performance

Recalling from Chapter 2 the importance of signaling legitimacy in overcoming newness, here we dig a little a deeper and provide more focus on distilling theory into evidence-based, actionable, and sequential advice for the bootstrapping entrepreneur. Since entrepreneurs must discover methods for communicating legitimizing signals to the customer even though they are saddled with substantial newness liabilities, taking a little time to begin sending strong, honest, positive signals in nascence is worth it. Ultimately, these signals must convey *size* and *age*—and the reliability and value that go along with them—to customers. To outline theoretically derived tactics for doing this, let us explore the model presented above by asking what legitimizing signals does the customer want to see?

Sending Legitimizing Signals

In contrast to financiers, customers are less likely to engage in active due diligence. This is typically because they do not have "skin in the game" in the same way that financiers do (Ardichvili, Cardozo, & Ray, 2003). While a financial investor—who is incurring monetary risk—is very likely to engage in thoroughly assessing a new venture to determine if the goals of an investor and entrepreneur are aligned, and to lessen moral hazard, a customer has less motivation—and fewer resources—to follow this procedure with the thoroughness required by due diligence. As such, customers generally will not legitimize a venture that forces them to engage in prolonged or in-depth research (Ashforth & Gibbs, 1990). These red flags ultimately decrease the chances of a positive legitimacy judgment.

At a minimum, the customer wants to have their needs met or pain relieved in a practical way. If entrepreneurs can send the signal that their offering solves a problem or fulfills a need for the customer, the likelihood that the individual will judge the product or service (and therefore the venture) as legitimate will increase.

Recall our earlier example of Under Armour. Kevin Plank realized early on that he was going to have to approach customers with legitimizing signals, but there was very little chance that customers would perceive legitimacy in this start-up in an industry where the likes of Nike, Reebok, and Adidas have big-time reputations. He knew, though, if he could get organized quickly and cheaply, and tap a few sports buddies for key contacts, he could gain some practical legitimacy—he felt strongly that his product would add value to the players on football teams.

More than this, though, customers want the new venture to be easily identifiable and understandable with an established firm or set of firms. For example, things like location become important. The premises must be located in a legitimate area; the building must be professional, well maintained, and nicely appointed. While the firm may offer a novel product, it must be easily understandable and similar to other reliable, valuable products.

Below, I outline three groups of activities that are most likely to assist the entrepreneurs in sending legitimizing signals. The first group, I term organizing activities, represents a collection of activities that "formalize" a venture early on. This formalization goes a long way toward establishing appropriateness in the eyes of customers. The second group addresses the strategic activities, including the business plan that will likely prove fruitful. The last group, termed capital gathering activities, directly focuses on the type and amount of capital—financial and otherwise—that the entrepreneur can access.

Organizing activities. First, entrepreneurs should get organized in nascence—literally. The advice here is largely targeted at helping the entrepreneur attain some base level of legitimacy from customers by sending strong signals that the company will add value to the customer and is unlikely to fail in the near term. The activities listed below serve to make information more symmetrical, and therefore instill confidence. This will also help down the road when the entrepreneur is seeking favorable investment terms.

Research indicates that the following organizing activities are the ones that are most likely to send legitimizing signals to customers (Eckhardt, Shane, & Delmar, 2006):

- Assemble a prototype—or minimally viable product (Reis, 2011). This also applies to service businesses. Have something tangible, or as close to tangible as possible, that allows the customer to envision themselves using the product or service. The challenge here will be doing this cheaply, but it is crucial.
- Complete all necessary tax forms. First, obtain an Employment Identification Number (EIN). Next, obtain necessary state and federal tax numbers. The website of the Small Business Administration (SBA) is a great resource here (www.sba.gov).
- Secure necessary permits and licenses. At a minimum, this likely includes obtaining a local business license and zoning permit. Again, the SBA website can help.
- Set up separate bank accounts. Simply opening an account that is separate from one's personal account will go a long way in establishing a separate entity and thereby some modicum of legitimacy. This will also help the entrepreneur limit liability if the time comes.
- Incorporate. Form something other than a sole proprietorship, whether that be an LLC, S-corp, C-corp or partnership. Research indicates that approximately 36 percent of start-ups form as sole proprietorships (Kauffman Firm Survey, 2008), when the advantages of organizing differently are well known (Shane, 2008). First, organizing in this way limits an entrepreneur's liability, even if it is not a foolproof way to do so. Second, these structures enhance legitimacy as stakeholders are more likely to view the firm as established (Delmar & Shane, 2004). The cost of organizing this is negligible; however, like many of these issues, bootstrapped entrepreneurs are simply less likely to be informed of value-adding techniques.

- Secure intellectual property. Assuming the entrepreneur can protect some form of the business concept this should be done to the extent possible. The patenting process is extremely costly and time consuming, but an alternative is applying for a provisional patent. Trademarks and copyrights are somewhat less involved. The U.S. Patent and Trademark Office website (http://www.uspto.gov/) is a helpful resource here.

- Prepare marketing materials. At a minimum, have business cards, brochures, and other written communication material professionally prepared. For many bootstrapped entrepreneurs, this material represents the face of the business at start-up. They are unlikely to be able to boast lavish locations, huge sponsorships, or legions of employees so this relatively minor expense can send a strong signal of legitimacy.

- Assemble an advisory committee. This is an enormously helpful tactic that is seldom discussed in the literature. An advisory committee has many advantages. The first is, obviously, high-quality advice from trusted mentors. The second is a greatly expanded network for the entrepreneur, as each advisor will have his or her own established network. The third reason is slightly more subtle and involves a "gray hair" signal. For young entrepreneurs, a more experienced board member can send an honest signal of age. It is important to remember that the entrepreneur and the firm are fused at this point, so the firm can add legitimacy to the entrepreneur and the entrepreneur can add legitimacy to the firm.

- Identify an accountant. As much as bootstrappers like to do it by themselves, this is one area that is best handled by the professionals. At a minimum, a bona fide and experienced accountant should file the entrepreneur's tax return. It is worth doing some research and finding an accountant that is experienced in assisting new and small businesses. To keep billable hours down, buy a financial software package.

- Identify an attorney. Similarly, invest some money in a good, small-business attorney and have the attorney read and approve your incorporation documents. While websites like nolo.com can be very helpful here, at some point all entrepreneurs will need an actual attorney.

Strategic activities. Write a plan even if you do not use it. To be clear: business plans are likely overrated in their ability to assist an entrepreneur during start-up. However, this does not mean that they are useless, and academic research is fairly definitive on the point that writing a business plan will lead to greater revenue and profitability for the entrepreneur's firm (Brinkmann, Grichnik, & Kapsa, 2010). This relation is present for two likely reasons: (1) a great deal of knowledge can be gathered in planning process, and (2) business plans serve as a valuable signal to customers and other stakeholders. Stakeholders expect to see new venture entrepreneurs with business plan in hand, and when absent, it appears inappropriate. The business plan does not necessarily need to be "full blown," but there are a number of valuable components—particularly for novice entrepreneurs who lack experience in the industry.

It is important to understand outcomes when considering business plan development. Business plans have one of two intended outcomes: (1) to attain legitimacy or (2) to assist in strategy crafting. The first may or may not be directly related to the second.

The first outcome involves an entirely different audience than the second. The most important implication of this statement is that the first outcome involves a marketing document, whereas the second involves a strategic document. In other words, the first is attempting to describe the firm in the most positive—but objective—manner possible, and the second is attempting to describe the firm in most realistic manner possible. These are two very different purposes and care should be taken not to confuse the two.

- First, define your business model. By business model, it is simply meant all the activities that are necessary for your new venture to convert supplies—including labor— into revenue (for a good analysis, see Porter, 1985). An entrepreneur might start by asking: where does money change hands? And then:

why would a customer pay for my product or service—what is the value-added? This will allow you to begin to understand and communicate supplies/suppliers and your ideal *target market*. Moreover, it will guide you in thinking about your operations and help you state your value-added criteria very clearly.

- Start out identifying a single group of customers for initial targeting, a single product or service. This, so-called, *first customer* approach can help an entrepreneur focus on a target market that is most likely to bear early fruit and generate much needed revenue as quickly as possible.
- Next, define your competitive advantage. What about your product or service is valuable to customers, difficult for competitors to imitate, and relatively rare?
- Develop a generic strategy. A broad strategy can go a long way. Bootstrappers often jump into the market and "pivot," but a little forethought as to how to compete (e.g., via cost or differentiation) will likely increase performance. Further to this point, start-up entrepreneurs want to strongly consider a differentiation strategy—a strategy based on offering a value-added difference to the identified target market, as opposed to a strategy based on offering the lowest price. This type of strategy will likely allow the entrepreneur to charge a higher price and thereby drive revenue. It is very difficult for new and small ventures to compete on cost, because this type of competition generally involves attaining economies of scale, and economies of scale generally involves having a large resource base.
- Engage in some industry analysis. At a minimum, define key competitors, barriers to entry, industry size, industry growth rate, and industry profitability.
- Set some general benchmarks and milestones.
- Guestimate profitability via a proforma income statement. It is a virtual surety that any and all proforma financial statements will be off the mark—probably by a wide margin. Again, though, this does not mean that they are without value. Drawing up a first-year income statement will force

the entrepreneur to put an estimate on number of customers, establish initial price points, and consider the multitude of expenses that will face the firm. More importantly, these numbers will allow the entrepreneur to establish initial metrics for breakeven, time until cash-positive, and burn rate. Also, from this analysis, the entrepreneur can get an idea of how much money that venture will need to stay afloat before it begins generating its own cash.

Capital-gathering activities. Gather and assess your resources—financial, human, and social. Does the entrepreneur possess some initial stock of capital? Let us assume that the entrepreneur is not independently wealthy, for this would take him out of the bootstrapped configuration because he would not have to engage in creative techniques to operate without capital. Initial capital stock includes more than just financial capital (Sarasvathy, 2001). Recall that broadly, capital can be categorized as financial, human, and social. Here, we move to consider ways that the entrepreneur human and social capital can help send legitimizing signals to customers.

Human capital. The first form of human capital is the entrepreneur him- or herself. Entrepreneurs may be able to leverage their knowledge or energy in a way that sends strong signals—so-called sweat equity, ultimately utilizing these softer forms of capital to attain hard financial capital. The founder and venture are largely indistinguishable from one another in the early going. As a result, the firm's legitimacy is heavily impacted by the founder's legitimacy.

Social capital. In addition, network depth and breadth (i.e., social capital) of the entrepreneur matters a great deal. In fact, social capital may be the entrepreneur's best bet for sending legitimizing signals to customers (Baron & Markman, 2000). Specifically, founders with higher levels of social capital will have a wider variety of individuals from whom to gather critical knowledge about exploiting market opportunities (Shane & Venkataraman, 2000). Due to their high level of knowledge about market opportunities, such founders should be better able to develop additional viable alternatives, which will in turn enhance their chances of successfully navigating the start-up process.

Empirical research indicates that new venture founders who discovered profitable opportunities tended to maintain more network relationships with individuals such as possible customers, financiers, and suppliers (Ozgen & Baron, 2007). Further, new ventures operated by founders with high levels of social capital tend to experience better firm performance (indicating that such firms were likely legitimized faster) than ventures operated by founders with weaker social networks (Davidsson & Honig, 2003).

To build this network, the entrepreneur must get out of the home, office, or garage. Before start-up is the prime time for networking. Develop relationships with key customers before hanging a shingle. It is wise to develop relationships before the need arises to ask for resources. These relationships will dramatically enhance chances for receiving those resources (Berger & Udell, 1995). Moreover, networking with no immediate "ask" is a much more natural, comfortable experience for both parties. Once you are in start-up mode, developing these relationships becomes trickier as friendly discussions become sales calls or pitches (Oneyah, Pesquera, & Ali, 2013).

Building this capital involves, but is absolutely not limited to, building your social media platform. As contacts are developed in person, they should be added to the entrepreneur's Twitter, LinkedIn, and/or Facebook networks. Social media will be an important resource as entrepreneurs market their businesses and having this established a priori will save valuable time when the chaos of start-up hits, but it is not a substitute for traditional networking.

For those who feel disconnected from the start-up communities in their respective area, there are a number of advisable ways to begin. First, locate the nearest Small Business Development Center (SBDC). SBDCs are operated by SBA to advise entrepreneurs and these organizations are often well connected with other valuable organizations in your area. Next, tap into the nearest college or university. These institutions often serve as entrepreneurial hubs for geographic areas.

In the end, it is clearly not the absence of financial capital that benefits the bootstrapped organization, it is the presence of human and social capital and the creativity and work ethic of the entrepreneur to mobilize these resource bases—long held by researchers to be a (if not the) critical resource for new ventures (Stam, 2013). If the entrepreneur can build these forms of capital without the use of external funds, bootstrapping becomes a much more manageable process.

Summary

The prescriptions above follow from signaling and legitimacy theories and essentially answer the question: what actions can an entrepreneur take to send signals of legitimacy, even though the entrepreneur has no legitimacy? The actions listed above can send strong signals of legitimacy by communicating that the new firm is larger and older than a stakeholder might otherwise perceive, in essence, overcoming the liabilities of newness.

As such, the central theme of this chapter is that time in nascence should be spent wisely. This book does take some issue with the recent movement toward lean start-ups and effectuation theories because these views tend to diminish the importance of the period of time before start-up, as though minimizing time in nascence to rush into start-up mode is, in and of itself, a valuable tactic. It is likely not, as research indicates that time in nascence is valuable (Shane, 2008). Having said that, entrepreneurs cannot stay in nascence forever; at some point, they must take the leap. But a handful of extremely impactful, activities, outlined above, in nascence can skyrocket an entrepreneur's chance of success. These steps will assist entrepreneurs by helping them bootstrap in a way that allows them to create wealth.

While time in start-up mode is generally limited—either the firm fails or grows out of this stage, time in nascence can be a longer period of time—an indeterminate period time really. Evidence suggests that there are many things that can be done to positively affect signal legitimacy on a bootstrapper's budget. These are the techniques were one will want to focus their time and effort.

As a final note, while the study of these relationships has progressed a great deal, the area is still young and certainly additional studies will follow that will further inform best practices.

CHAPTER 6

Typologies for Strategic Bootstrapping Success

About This Chapter

Bootstrapping is not for the fainthearted. Growing without external finance is a challenging endeavor and certainly many attempts will fail. However, in keeping with the tone of Chapter 5, the entrepreneur can make decisions to greatly enhance their chances of success. Strategic bootstrapping is offered as a nostrum by outlining ways in which entrepreneurs may use the resources at hand in such a way that one can quickly attain legitimacy, break even, and grow so that bootstrapping—at least the onerous parts—will no longer be a necessity. This final chapter endeavors to further distill the points presented in previous chapters into the most salient advice.

Moving away from the specific advice offered in Chapter 5, though, this final chapter considers broad types of firms and behaviors that generally work for bootstrappers. This chapter considers structuring the firm and the entrepreneur's behavior in ways that are likely to mesh well with a resource-constrained situation. Below, I outline four typologies: Two of these outline types of entrepreneur behavior and the other two outline business models. My stance is this: if entrepreneurs can engage in one (or both) of these behavioral paradigms and choose one (or both) of these ideal business models, they can greatly enhance their chances of success.

On the other hand, if the entrepreneur chooses not to engage in these typologies, research suggests that they may be setting themselves up for failure. For example, the two behavioral types below involve a heavy dose of relationship building, interaction, and sharing. Research indicates that many entrepreneurs actually do the opposite. That is, they are secretive lone wolves who engage in little relationship building (Aldrich & Carter, 2004).

Chapter 4 presented typologies of both bootstrapping techniques and motivations. The typologies presented here differ from those presented in Chapter 4 in at least three ways:

- First, the typologies presented in Chapter 4 were empirically derived—strictly speaking, they are taxonomies. The models presented below are literature based, but have not been subjected to grouping procedures (e.g., factor analysis).
- Second, the typologies discussed in Chapter 4 describe how different entrepreneurs *actually* bootstrap—it is positivist. The typology below is normative. That is, my typology attempts to prescribe what entrepreneurs *should* do to succeed as bootstrappers, as opposed to what they actually do.
- Finally, the types below may overlap. Since these are not empirically derived paradigms, they are not necessarily orthogonal.

These typologies draw on substantial theory and research, as presented in the preceding chapters. Ultimately these are my strong, evidenced-based opinions on how bootstrappers should launch.

Strategic Bootstrapping—Behavioral Typologies

Throughout this book, a number of positive types of behavior for entrepreneurs have been discussed, but here I recount and further highlight two behavior typologies that have been shown to be the most helpful for strategic bootstrappers. Specifically, I will spend time drilling down on the behaviors of networking and sharing and elucidate how those behaviors can send signals that attract customers while keeping costs and expenses down.

(1) The hyper-networked entrepreneur

In explaining this type, I will build on the advice from the last chapter on social capital. All entrepreneurs should network to build social capital, but some entrepreneurs are able to become "hyper-networked." The hyper-networked entrepreneur is able to develop and leverage relationships so well, that attempting to attract outside capital actually becomes unnecessary and possibly detrimental to firm performance.

As an example, consider Veritas Prep, a firm that helps aspiring graduate students prepare for standardized tests like the LSAT and GMAT. Using the team members and professors associated with well-known universities (Yale, University of Missouri, Arizona State), founder Chad Troutwine (a graduate of the three universities) was able to leverage these contacts to ease the transition from nascence to start-up (http://www.entrepreneur.com/video/217619). Using only modest funds from a business plan competition victory, Troutwine attracted a cofounder with coding skills (Yale alumnus Markus Moberg) and was able to hire teachers for his classes from the graduate student body at these schools. He also needed permission to use and reserve classrooms on campus. University officials are often reluctant to do this for students, but will for faculty members. Similarly, he was able to develop his business plan while finishing his MBA—the whole time obtaining highly valuable advice from knowledgeable and well-connected professors and alumni.

"Network" in this context refers to an entrepreneur's social network—their ability to make and maintain valuable, trusting contacts with others. Most new venture entrepreneurs struggle in this regard and must rely on "strangers" to assist them (Aldrich & Carter, 2004). In general, strangers are less likely to endorse an unfamiliar entrepreneur than are trusted members of a network (Jones & Jayawarna, 2010). While many entrepreneurs see themselves as solitary cowboys, networked entrepreneurs understand that entrepreneurship involves actively and successfully engaging customers, and this is much easier to do if one has a large and "valuable" network.

How does a network help an entrepreneur send high-quality signals? First and foremost, entrepreneurs' network members can connect them to prospective customers (De Carolis, Litzky, & Eddleston, 2009). Since entrepreneurs have a chief goal after launch of securing paying customers, obviously, they must engage them in some way. Clearly, there are myriad ways to go about this (e.g., advertising, cold calls, etc.), but the most impactful is word-of-mouth, or referral. Assuming that entrepreneurs do not have all the necessary customers in their network, they will need to reach out to strangers. While a prospective customer is unlikely to quickly endorse an unknown entrepreneur, with an unknown venture, that customer will be far more likely to endorse a new venture that has been referred by a trusted colleague or friend. In this way, entrepreneurs are able to "borrow" legitimacy from legitimate others in their network.

A larger network simply gives the entrepreneur more word-of-mouth advocates in the marketplace. This type of entrepreneur essentially makes up for the lack of financial capital with social capital, or least leverages social capital to gain financial capital. It reduces newness a great deal because the customer is not necessarily judging the entrepreneur; the customer is judging the referrer.

To be successful in this typology, entrepreneurs will want to be very deliberate in mapping out their current network, as well as mapping out their ideal network. Mr. Troutwine, for example, knew that he needed successful and esteemed academics to teach his classes if he was to gain credibility for his start-up. He did this by identifying and engaging them from the start.

For some entrepreneurs, building a legitimizing hyper-network will be far more difficult—not all of us attended Ivy League universities. However, within a locality or industry sector, entrepreneurs may be able to become connected with many influential players. This will likely involve identifying key players and then thoughtfully putting oneself in situations to come in contact with these players. While this may smack of Machiavellianism, it is a necessary part of entrepreneurship, particularly when bootstrapping.

As a note on this type, the rapid emergence of social media has not fundamentally changed the dynamic of networking in this way, but it has made it somewhat easier for the savvy entrepreneur to establish and grow a network. Portals like LinkedIn, Facebook, and Reddit can leverage face-to-face relationships in a way not possible before these virtual networking tools.

(2) The sharing entrepreneur

This behavior displayed by this type of entrepreneur builds on the notion of joint utilization introduced in Chapter 4. These entrepreneurs seek out partnerships with those who will share expenses and assist in driving revenues. Similar to networked entrepreneurs, this type is relationship oriented, but in contrast to sharing entrepreneurs they are more transactional—they are seeking a fairly specific cost savings or revenue producer. Possibly, the most straightforward example is the entrepreneur who chooses to colocate with others in an incubator or accelerator. It is important that the customer either cannot perceive the sharing or will actually value the sharing. Otherwise sharing will likely send a negative signal, as it is suggestive of a cash-strapped, struggling company. However, done properly, techniques that comprise sharing have the ability to send signals of size and age, while containing costs.

Jenni's Splendid Ice Creams began operations in the North Market incubator in Columbus, OH in 2002. The North Market has a focus on food business start-ups and has approximately 35 of these businesses in the incubator (http://www.entrepreneur.com/article/219485). Founder Jenni Britton Bauer was able to leverage not only some shared back office operations (e.g., supplies, secretarial, bookkeeping) with other businesses, but also had access to the incubator's board members which include area business leaders who are experts in marketing, retailing, business law, and accounting. The North Market is supported by tenant rents, paid parking in its lots, and a series of communal fundraising events.

The incubator provided other advantages as well. By colocating with similar businesses, Ms. Britton Bauer was able to constantly taste and experiment with the different ingredients offered by these businesses. Possibly more importantly, by choosing high-quality food-related business to house in the incubator; the North Market attracts more than a million potential customers each year. Because of all these advantages, Jenni's Splendid Ice Creams was able to graduate from the incubator, and this wholesale and retail business now has eight locations in the Columbus area.

Recounting from Chapter 4, the research is fairly clear on this point—sharing resources with other entrepreneurs and firms is wise. Sharing space, employees, equipment, and purchases satisfies our two apparently opposing criteria for strategic bootstrapping—it contains cost by pooling them in a "quasi-economies of scale" condition, while allowing entrepreneurs to grow revenue.

Another common way that sharing entrepreneurs bootstrap strategically is by bartering. These entrepreneurs attain many of their required resources by trading goods and services with others, without exchanging money (it is worth noting that barter transactions are not tax free and entrepreneurs should include the fair market value of goods/services received as gross income). In this way, they are able to save valuable cash and instead use it to send honest and valuable signals to customers. Again, it should be noted that bartering, in general, will not be perceived as a legitimizing signal by customers. Accordingly, the entrepreneur will want to be very careful bartering with primary customers. However, if the customer base never perceives this behind-the-scenes bartering, then this broad strategy can work and is quite savvy. There even exist online bartering clubs that can be very helpful for cash-strapped entrepreneurs. *BarterQuest* is one such example. The rise of these portals has made bartering as popular as ever (American express OPEN survey).

Strategic Bootstrapping—Business Model Typologies

This section more heavily considers firm-level considerations. While start-up entrepreneurs are virtually always inextricably intertwined with their ventures, some issues are more firm oriented than entrepreneur oriented. The models presented below again offer the opportunity to send high-quality signals while keeping cash outflow low.

(1) The digital entrepreneur

This broad type refers to entrepreneurial ventures that primarily exist in virtual form. Airbnb, Uber, and Wikipedia are all examples of digital enterprises. The product/service is delivered online or facilitated heavily by the Internet—this includes apps for tablets and smart phones. This online content delivery allows entrepreneurs to more fully separate themselves and their new ventures from the merits of the product/service. With a well-designed site or application, the youth and size of the firm will never be perceived—a web site or application developed by a start-up can appear very similar to one developed by a Fortune 500 company. As long as the customer perceives value in the offering, it does not matter that the firm is 3 months old and the entrepreneur is a high school sophomore with $17 in the bank. It is simply unlikely that the customer will have this knowledge, or work hard to gain it (Bitektine, 2011).

Web and application-based businesses often have an easier time sending signals of viability, because these signals are not as costly. This fact has given rise to a very interesting new reality for bootstrapping new ventures: A web presence can appear legitimate with limited funds. The literature has long maintained that a key way that firms attain legitimacy is by mimicking practices and structures of legitimate firms—this is termed *isomorphism* (Suchman, 1995). For most start-ups, mimicking large firms is exceptionally challenging, involving considerable expense. This is far more attainable in a virtual setting.

This is much harder to pull off with a bricks and mortar location. Certainly, for the digital entrepreneur, there will be investments in design and coding personnel, but launching a Web site or app can be a more piecemeal launch, which allows the entrepreneur to fund some of the launch with revenues from the young organization. The rapid rise of the digital entrepreneur is a likely reason why the Lean Startup (Ries, 2011) methodology has become so popular, as the fundamentals of that methodology work very well in a web or application-based setting.

This can be made even more cost-effective if the entrepreneur possesses design and/or coding skills. While not simple, entrepreneurs can learn to code (including design training) relatively inexpensively through online training tools such as *Codecademy*, *Starter League*, and *Iron Yard*. In addition, many of the skills and tasks needed to launch and maintain a high-quality Web site can be outsourced or subcontracted. Portals like *Elance*, *GetaFreeLancer*, and *oDesk* are all resources for entrepreneurs to find programmers and web designers.

(2) The fragmented entrepreneur

Fragmented industries are prime contexts for bootstrapping. Fragmented industries are those that have many small competitors and very few large competitors. Examples would be landscaping/lawn service, auto repair, hair salons, and restaurants. These markets may be saturated with competitors, but because these competitors are relatively unsophisticated and informal, best practices have not necessarily been developed and substandard, inconsistent pricing and quality is the norm.

In a market where the vast majority of competitors are ineffective, inefficient or both, the possibility exists that a superior firm can grow and create wealth by consolidating and formalizing a fragmented industry through hard work and superior execution (Bhide, 1992). Moreover, because of low-entry barriers, expenses can be kept low.

Essentially, in fragmented industries, there are very few firms sending valuable signals to customers, therefore it is relatively easy and inexpensive for capable entrepreneurs to enter such a market and begin sending these signals. With a few notable exceptions (Dollinger, 1990), the academic literature is interestingly quiet on the subject of fragmented industries, likely because the vast majority of firms are not high performers and not particularly innovative or interesting. However, it is known that some firms are able to exploit these markets at start-up and achieve success.

Recall the earlier example of 1-800-GOT-JUNK. This firm was able to enter a fragmented industry and simply outhustle and out-compete rough-around-the-edges rivals. Like most fragmented industries, the margins in the junk-removal industry were not attractive enough to attract large, sophisticated, well-resourced firms; therefore, only small, ineffective competitors remained when Brian Scudamore entered in 1989. Engaging some due diligence, Scudamore estimated that there were some 2,000 "guys with trucks" in his area removing junk. He also realized that none of them performed the service very well. The industry was rife with unreliable service and inconsistent pricing. The opportunity to beat these competitors with superior professionalism and hustle existed.

It is important to be clear on this point: On average, fragmented industries are not good industries for creating wealth. These industries tend to have much lower revenue and profitability and much higher failure rates than others (Dess, 1987). But there are industries—or subindustries—that are "diamonds in the rough." Accordingly, entrepreneurs should be diligent in researching the competition and assessing the nature of the industry before launching.

Points of Caution and Tactics to Avoid

When one considers the four typologies above, it should be clear that bootstrapping, even strategic bootstrapping, is a short-term endeavor—it is a means to an end. That is, at some point of development, firms will want to attract some outside funding (recall static trade-off from Chapter 4) to take advantage of opportunities and reduce risk.

With that in mind, allow me to highlight a few important points of caution when considering the strategic bootstrapping approach.

- Consider the ethical implications of bootstrapping. Specifically, here I am referring to the tendency and allure of lying to stakeholders during start-up. While this tendency exists for any prelegitimate entrepreneur, bootstrapped entrepreneurs are uniquely challenged in this regard (Rutherford, Buller, & Stebbins, 2009). The reason for this is the "chicken-and-egg" scenario laid out earlier—customers simply do not want to endorse a venture that has not been endorsed by others. The hallmarks of being new are "red flags" that work against new ventures. As a result, the temptation will be strong for the entrepreneur to exaggerate the size, age, and abilities of the venture. While the mantra may be "fake it till you make it," entrepreneurs must be sure not to violate social contracts made with stakeholders.
- Collect accounts receivable. This may seem obvious, but it is certainly not uncommon for new ventures to grow themselves out of business. As noted many times, revenue is not equal to cash. Entrepreneurs must be diligent in collecting actual cash from customers. A few delayed payments can spell failure for an otherwise successful enterprise.
- Assess exit barriers. Even with the principles outlined in this text, the chances that a hardworking, capable entrepreneur

will fail are substantial. There are simply so many unknowable factors that can doom a start-up, that they cannot all be predicted or removed. Accordingly entrepreneurs want to be sure that they can jump ship with as little financial damage as possible. Remember, bootstrapping means that entrepreneurs shoulder all the risk of failure. Therefore, an appraisal of exit barriers must be made. Essentially, this involves estimating the difficulty and expense of dissolving the business.

- Keep an eye on the "threshold." Once new ventures have crossed the legitimacy threshold—that is, attained a base level of legitimacy—entrepreneurs will likely have to switch their attention from acquiring customers to effectively managing the enterprise. Once the venture has been adequately legitimized by cash-granting stakeholders, the venture will begin to grow. However, with growth, the venture will most likely have other internal issues such as human resource management and logistical problems that are less critical to prelegitimate ventures, but of paramount importance to growing ventures (Rutherford, Buller, & Stebbins, 2009). When an entrepreneur's problems begin coming from inside (e.g., employees, logistics) rather than outside (e.g., customers), a major shift is like coming. Entrepreneurs should not shy away from seeking external professional help e.g., consultants at this point.

Summary

The strategic bootstrapping approach involves utilizing one's time and creativity to be frugal and grow revenue, rather than wasting it solely on saving money. When entrepreneurs are devising ways to save money they should also be devising ways to simultaneously drive revenues—this is an effective use of the entrepreneur's time and will maximize their chance of creating wealth and exiting bootstrapping. Time spent solely on saving money may prolong the existence of the firm; however, that existence will likely be a meager one. This is because the business is being starved from what it needs most—cash—and the entrepreneur should be focused on driving quantity (i.e., selling products/services) and driving prices up via differentiation. The actions taken to drive revenues are externally facing duties, while too often cost containment is an internally facing duty. Start-up entrepreneurs are successful when they engage external stakeholders that grant cash to firm—customers and financiers. It is hoped the typologies presented in this chapter will allow entrepreneurs to accomplish these two critical, but often paradoxical, goals.

This typology is not exhaustive. It is likely that other typologies for successful bootstrapping exist, however, based on the extant work by academics and practitioners, it is believed that these four are the most salient and promising. Accordingly, only after careful consideration and research should these typologies be rejected in favor of an alternative.

References

Chapter 1

Accion San Diego. (2011, April). April Inspirational Client Spotlight: Lidia Calzado. *Microfinance Matters.* Retrieved from http://www.accionsandiego .org/documents/AprilNewsletter.pdf

Aldrich, H. E., & Martinez, M. A. (2001). Many are called, but few are chosen: An evolutionary perspective for the study of entrepreneurship. *Entrepreneurship Theory and Practice, 25*(4), 41–56.

Barney, J. (1991). Firm resources and sustained competitive advantage. *Journal of Management, 17*(1), 99–120.

Butler, A., Fauver, L., & McDonald, M. (2013). Local Economic Consequences of Stock Market Listing Changes. *University of Tennessee Working Paper.*

Carpentier, C., & Suret, J. M. (2006). Bypassing the financial growth cycle: Evidence from capital pool companies. *Journal of Business Venturing, 21*(1), 45–73.

Cooper, H. M. (1988). The structure of knowledge synthesis. *Knowledge in Society, 1*(1), 104–126.

Freear, J., Sohl, J. E., & Wetzel Jr, W. E. (1995). Angels: Personal investors in the venture capital market. *Entrepreneurship & Regional Development, 7*(1), 85–94.

Freear, J., Sohl, J., & Wetzel, W. (1990). Raising venture capital: Entrepreneurs' view of the process. In *Frontiers of Entrepreneurship Research 1990.* Babson Park, MA: Babson College. 223–237.

Goodman, M. (2013, December 23). A Chain of Brain-Fitness Stores Gets Big-Time Funding. *Entrepreneur.* Retrieved from http://www.entrepreneur.com/ article/229372

Grichnik, D., & Singh, L. (2010). Resource bootstrapping of nascent entrepreneurs: Conscious entrepreneurial decision or forced reaction? *Frontiers of Entrepreneurship Research, 30*(12), 3.

Kim, M., Lee, J. H., Koh, H., Lee, S. Y., Jang, C., Chung, C. J., . . . & Chung, J. (2006). Inhibition of ERK-MAP kinase signaling by RSK during Drosophila development. *The EMBO Journal, 25*(13), 3056–3067.

Knaup, A. E. (2005). Survival and longevity in the business employment dynamics data. *Monthly Labor Review, 128,* 50.

McDougall, P., & Robinson, R. B. (1990). New venture strategies: An empirical identification of eight 'archetypes' of competitive strategies for entry. *Strategic Management Journal, 11*(6), 447–467.

Neeley, L., & Van Auken, H. (2010). Differences between female and male entrepreneurs' use of bootstrap financing. *Journal of Developmental Entrepreneurship, 15*(01), 19–34.

Neely, L., & Van Auken, H. (2012). An examination of small firm bootstrap financing and use of debt. *Journal of Developmental Entrepreneurship, 17*(01).

Penrose, E. T. (1959). *The Theory of the Growth of the Firm.* New York: John WileyGreen Cleaning Magazine. (2013, October 2). People We Love: Eco Me. Retrieved September 2, 2014, from http://www.greencleaningmagazine.com/people-we-love-eco-me/

PrivCo. (n.d.). Gerbing's Heated Clothing, Inc. Retrieved August 26, 2014, from http://www.privco.com/private-company/gerbings-heated-clothing-inc

Ranger-Moore, J. (1997). Bigger may be better, but is older wiser? Organizational age and size in the New York life insurance industry. *American Sociological Review, 62*(2), 903–920.

Shane, S. (2008). *The Illusions of Entrepreneurship.* New Haven, CT: Yale University Press.

Shepherd, D. A., & Zacharakis, A. (2003). A new venture's cognitive legitimacy: An assessment by customers. *Journal of Small Business Management, 41*(2), 148–167.

Singh, K., Ang, S. H., & Leong, S. M. (2003). Increasing replication for knowledge accumulation in strategy research. *Journal of Management, 29*(4), 533–549.

Sohl, J. (2003). The private equity market in the USA: Lessons from volatility. *Venture Capital: An International Journal of Entrepreneurial Finance, 5*(1), 29–46.

Chapter 2

Bitektine, A. (2011). Toward a theory of social judgments of organizations: The case of legitimacy, reputation, and status. *Academy of Management Review, 36*(1), 151–179.

Govardhan, R., & Williamson, C. H. K. (2000). Modes of vortex formation and frequency response of a freely vibrating cylinder. *Journal of Fluid Mechanics, 420*, 85–130.

Hannan, M. T., & Freeman, J. (1988). The ecology of organizational mortality: American labor unions, 1836–1985. *American Journal of Sociology,* 25–52.

Jawahar, I. M., & McLaughlin, G. L. (2001). Toward a descriptive stakeholder theory: An organizational life cycle approach. *Academy of Management Review, 26*(3), 397–414.

Kawasaki, G. (2004). *The Art of the Start: The Time-Tested, Battle-Hardened Guide for Anyone Starting Anything.* New York, NY: Penguin.

Kuratko, D., & Hodgetts, R. (2006). *Entrepreneurship: Theory, Process, Practice.* (7th ed.). Mason, OH: Thomson South-Western.

PrivCo. (n.d.). Airbnb, Inc. Retrieved August 26, 2014, from http://www.privco.com/private-company/airbnb

The Profit. (2014). Planet Popcorn—The Profit CNBC Season 1 Episode 3. Retrieved from http://www.theprofitfans.com/2014/planet-popcorn-the-profit-cnbc-season-1-episode-3.html

Rosch, E. (1978). *Principles of Categorization*, in Rosch, E. & Lloyd, B.B. (eds). *Cognition and Categorization*, Hillsdale, NJ: Lawrence Erlbaum Associates.

Rutherford, M. W., Buller, P. F., & Stebbins, J. M. (2009). Ethical considerations of the legitimacy lie. *Entrepreneurship Theory and Practice, 33*(4), 949–964.

Stinchcombe, A. L. (1965). Social structure and organizations. In March, J.G. *Handbook of Organizations.* Chicago: Rand McNally. pp. 142–193.

Wasserman, N., Nazeeri, F., & Anderson, K. (2012, February 4). *A 'Rich-vs.-King' Approach to Term Sheet Negotiations.* (Harvard Business School Entrepreneurial Management Case Note 810-119). Boston, MA: Harvard Business School.

Zimmerman, M. A., & Zeitz, G. J. (2002). Beyond survival: Achieving new venture growth by building legitimacy. *Academy of Management Review, 27*(3), 414–431.

Chapter 3

Angel Capital Association. (n.d.). Act Now: Protect Angel Startup Funding. Retrieved September 1, 2014, from http://www.angelcapitalassociation.org/aca-public-policy-protect-angel-funding/

Akerlof, G. A. (1970). The market for "lemons": Quality uncertainty and the market mechanism. *Quarterly Journal of Economics, 84*(3), 488–500.

Alsos, G. A., Isaksen, E. J., & Ljunggren, E. (2006). New venture financing and subsequent business growth in men- and women-led businesses. *Entrepreneurship Theory and Practice, 30*(5), 667–686.

AngelList. (n.d.). Retrieved August 29, 2014, from https://angel.co/

Argosy Private Equity. (n.d.). Investment Focus. Retrieved August 27, 2014, from http://www.argosyprivateequity.com/about-argosy/investment-criteria/

Austin, S. (2011). Airbnb: From Y Combinator to $112M Funding in Three Years. Retrieved August 27, 2014, from http://blogs.wsj.com/venturecapital/2011/07/25/airbnb-from-y-combinator-to-112m-funding-in-three-years/

Barnett, C. (2014, May 1). $2B Facebook Acquisition Raises Question: Is Equity Crowdfunding Better? Retrieved September 1, 2014, from http://www.forbes.com/sites/chancebarnett/2014/05/01/2-billion-facebook-acquisition-raises-question-is-equity-crowdfunding-better/

Berger, A., & Udell, G. (1998). The economics of small business finance: The roles of private equity and debt markets in the financial growth cycle. *Journal of Banking & Finance, 22*(6), 613–673.

Bhide, A. (1992). Bootstrap finance: The art of start-ups. *Harvard Business Review, 70*(6), 109–117.

Brealey, R., & Myers, S. (1991). *Principles of Corporate Finance*. (4th ed.). New York, NY: McGraw-Hill.

Buss, D. (2014, June 20). Unlikely Luxury: $150 Floor Mats for Cars. Retrieved September 1, 2014, from http://forbesindia.com/article/cross-border/unlikely-luxury-$150-floor-mats-for-cars/38046/1

Deeds, D., DeCarolis, D. M., & Chaganti, R. (1995). Predictors of capital structure in small ventures. *Entrepreneurship Theory and Practice, 20*(2), 7–18.

Ebben, J. J. (2009). Bootstrapping and the financial condition of small firms. *International Journal of Entrepreneurial Behaviour & Research, 15*(4), 346–363.

Forbes. (n.d.). America's Most Promising Companies: The Top 25 of 2014. Retrieved September 1, 2014, from http://www.forbes.com/pictures/elld45efeih/fuhu/

Garage Technology Ventures. (n.d.). About Us. Retrieved August 27, 2014, from http://www.garage.com/about/

Gregory, B. T., Rutherford, M. W., Oswald, S., & Gardiner, L. (2005). An empirical investigation of the growth cycle theory of small firm financing. *Journal of Small Business Management, 43*(4), 382–392.

Juetten, M. (2014). JOBS Act and Crowdfunding: Will They Finally "#ReleaseTheRules"? *Forbes*. Retrieved from http://www.forbes.com/sites/maryjuetten/2014/08/21/jobs-act-and-crowdfunding-will-they-finally-releasetherules/

Modigliani, F., & Miller, M. H. (1958). The cost of capital, corporation finance and the theory of investment. *American Economic Review, 49*(4), 261–297.

Pozin, I. (2014). 3 Things to Know about Corporate Venture Capital. *Inc.* Retrieved from http://www.inc.com/ilya-pozin/3-things-to-know-corporate-venture-capital.html

Puri, M., & Zarutskie, R. (2012). On the life cycle dynamics of venture-capital-and non-venture-capital-financed firms. *Journal of Finance, 67*(6), 2247–2293.

Rutherford, M. W., Coombes, S. M. T., Mazzei, M. J. (2012). The impact of bootstrapping on new venture performance and survival: A longitudinal analysis. *Frontiers of Entrepreneurship Research, 32*(12), 4.

Shane, S. A. (2008). *The Illusions of Entrepreneurship: The Costly Myths that Entrepreneurs, Investors, and Policy Makers Live By*. New Haven, CT: Yale University Press.

Shane, S., & Venkataraman, S. (2000). The promise of entrepreneurship as a field of research. *Academy of Management Review, 25*(1), 217–226.

Thomson Reuters. (2014, March). *National Venture Capital Association Yearbook 2004*. (17th ed.). New York: NY. Author.

U.S. Securities and Exchange Commission. (n.d.). Accredited Investors. Retrieved from http://www.sec.gov/answers/accred.htm

Vinturella, J. B., & Erickson, S. M. (2003). *Raising Entrepreneurial Capital.* Waltham: MA. Academic Press.

Wasserman, N. (2008). Revisiting the strategy, structure, and performance paradigm: The case of venture capital. *Organization Science, 19*(2), 241–259.

Weaver, J. (2013, September 18). Miami Businessman Claudio Osorio Gets 12 Years in Prison for Fraud Conviction—Miami-Dade—Miami Herald.com. Retrieved September 1, 2014, from http://www.miamiherald.com/2013/09/17/3632865/miami-businessman-claudio-osorio.html

Winborg, J., & Landström, H. (2000). Financial bootstrapping in small businesses: Examining small business managers' resource acquisition behaviors. *Journal of Business Venturing, 16*(3), 235–254.

Chapter 4

Barker, E. (2002, February 1). Start with Nothing. Retrieved August 30, 2014, from http://www.inc.com/magazine/20020201/23855.html

Blanchflower, D., & Oswald, A. J. (1990). *What Makes an Entrepreneur? Evidence on Inheritance and Capital Constraints.* (NBER Working Paper No. w3252). Cambridge, MA: National Bureau of Economic Research.

Carpentier, C., & Suret, J. M. (2006). Bypassing the financial growth cycle: Evidence from capital pool companies. *Journal of Business Venturing, 21*(1), 45–73.

Carter, R. B., & Van Auken, H. (2005). Bootstrap financing and owners' perceptions of their business constraints and opportunities. *Entrepreneurship & Regional Development, 17*(2), 129–144.

Double Line Partners Goes from Zero to $20 Million in Five Years–Silicon-Hills. (n.d.). Retrieved August 30, 2014, from http://www.siliconhillsnews.com/2014/06/07/double-line-partners-goes-from-zero-to-20-million-in-five-years/

Ebben, J., & Johnson, A. (2006). Bootstrapping in small firms: An empirical analysis of change over time. *Journal of Business Venturing, 21*(6), 851–865.

Forbes, D. P. (2005). Are some entrepreneurs more overconfident than others? *Journal of Business Venturing, 20*(5), 623–640.

Grichnik, D., & Singh, L. (2010). Resource bootstrapping of nascent entrepreneurs: Conscious entrepreneurial decision or forced reaction? *Frontiers of Entrepreneurship Research, 30*(12), 3.

Hessels, J., Van Gelderen, M., & Thurik, R. (2008). Entrepreneurial aspirations, motivations, and their drivers. *Small Business Economics, 31*(3), 323–339.

Kawaguchi, D. (2008). Self-employment rents: Evidence from job. *Hitotsubashi Journal of Economics*, *49*(1), 35–45.

Korkeamaki, T. P., & Rutherford, M. W. (2006). Industry effects and banking relationship as determinants of small firm capital structure decisions. *Journal of Entrepreneurial Finance*, *11*(1), 23–38.

Linderman, M. (2011). Bootstrapped, Profitable, & Proud: Goldstar. Signal v. Noise. Retrieved from https://signalvnoise.com/posts/2841-bootstrapped-profitable-proud-goldstar-

Lorek, L. (2014, June 7). Double Line Partners Goes from Zero to $20 Million in Five Years—SiliconHills. Retrieved August 30, 2014, from http://www.siliconhillsnews.com/2014/06/07/double-line-partners-goes-from-zero-to-20-million-in-five-years/

Masulis, R. W. (1980). The effects of capital structure change on security prices: A study of exchange offers. *Journal of Financial Economics*, *8*(2), 139–178.

Patel, P.C., Fiet, J.O., & Sohl, J.E. (2011). Bootstrapping through strategic alliances to enhance new venture growth. *International Small Business Journal*, *29*(5), 421–447.

Quackenbush, J. (2010). Crushpad to Move to Napa Valley. Retrieved August 30, 2014, from http://www.northbaybusinessjournal.com/18269/crushpad-to-move-to-napa-valley/

Robb, A., & Farhat, J. (2013). An Overview of the Kauffman Firm Survey: Results from 2011 Business Activities. (SSRN 2055265). Retrieved from http://papers.ssrn.com/sol3/papers.cfm?abstract_id=2055265

Scherr, F. C., & Hulburt, H. M. (2001). The debt maturity structure of small firms. *Financial Management*, *30*(1), 85–111.

Shane, S. A. (2008). *The Illusions of Entrepreneurship: The Costly Myths that Entrepreneurs, Investors, and Policy Makers Live By*. New Haven, CT: Yale University Press.

Shinal, J. (2011, February 4). Pandora Workers Walked the Long Start-Up Road. Retrieved August 30, 2014, from http://www.marketwatch.com/story/pandora-workers-walked-the-long-start-up-road-2011-02-04

Winborg, J. (2009). Use of financial bootstrapping in new businesses: A question of last resort? *Venture Capital*, *11*(1), 71–83.

Chapter 5

Ardichvili, A., Cardozo, R., & Ray, S. (2003). A theory of entrepreneurial opportunity identification and development. *Journal of Business Venturing*, *18*(1), 105–123.

Ashforth, B. E., & Gibbs, B. W. (1990). The double-edge of organizational legitimation. *Organization Science*, *1*(2), 177–194.

Baron, R. A., & Markman, G. D. (2000). Beyond social capital: How social skills can enhance entrepreneurs' success. *Academy of Management Executive, 14*(1), 106–116.

Berger, A. N., & Udell, G. F. (1995). Relationship lending and lines of credit in small firm finance. *Journal of Business, 68*(3), 351–381.

Brinckmann, J., Grichnik, D., & Kapsa, D. (2010). Should entrepreneurs plan or just storm the castle? A meta-analysis on contextual factors impacting the business planning–performance relationship in small firms. *Journal of Business Venturing, 25*(1), 24–40.

Carter, R. B., & Van Auken, H. (2005). Bootstrap financing and owners' perceptions of their business constraints and opportunities. *Entrepreneurship & Regional Development, 17*(2), 129–144.

Davidsson, P., & Honig, B. (2003). The role of social and human capital among nascent entrepreneurs. *Journal of Business Venturing, 18*(3), 301–331.

Delmar, F., & Shane, S. (2004). Legitimating first: Organizing activities and the survival of new ventures. *Journal of Business Venturing, 19*(3), 385–410.

Eckhardt, J. T., Shane, S., & Delmar, F. (2006). Multistage selection and the financing of new ventures. *Management Science, 52*(2), 220–232.

Kauffman Firm Survey. (2008, March). Results from the Baseline and First Follow-Up Surveys. Retrieved from http://papers.ssrn.com/sol3/papers.cfm?abstract_id=1098173

Kawaguchi, D. (2002). *Compensating Wage Differentials among Self-employed Workers: Evidence from Job Satisfaction Scores.* (ISER Discussion Paper No. 568). Osaka, Japan: Institute of Social and Economic Research, Osaka University.

Mintzberg, H., & Waters, J. A. (1985). Of strategies, deliberate and emergent. *Strategic Management Journal, 6*(3), 257–272.

Moskowitz, T. J., & Vissing-Jorgensen, A. (2002). *The Returns to Entrepreneurial Investment: A Private Equity Premium Puzzle?* (NBER Working Paper No. w8876). Cambridge, MA: National Bureau of Economic Research.

Onyemah, V., Pesquera, M. R., & Ali, A. (2013). What entrepreneurs get wrong. *Harvard Business Review, 91*(5), 74–79.

Ozgen, E., & Baron, R. A. (2007). Social sources of information in opportunity recognition: Effects of mentors, industry networks, and professional forums. *Journal of Business Venturing, 22*(2), 174–192.

Porter, M. E. (1985). Competitive Advantage: Creating and Sustaining Superior Performance. New York, NY: Free Press.

Reis, C. (2011). Entrepreneurial labor and capital taxation. *Macroeconomic Dynamics, 15*(03), 326–335.

Rutherford, M. W., Coombes, S. M., & Mazzei, M. J. (2012). The impact of bootstrapping on new venture performance and survival: A longitudinal analysis. *Frontiers of Entrepreneurship Research, 32*(12), 4.

Sarasvathy, S. D. (2001). Causation and effectuation: Toward a theoretical shift from economic inevitability to entrepreneurial contingency. *Academy of Management Review, 26*(2), 243–263.

Shane, S. A. (2008). *The Illusions of Entrepreneurship: The Costly Myths that Entrepreneurs, Investors, and Policy Makers Live By.* New Haven, CT: Yale University Press.

Shane, S., & Venkataraman, S. (2000). The promise of entrepreneurship as a field of research. *Academy of Management Review, 25*(1), 217–226.

Stam, E. (2013). Knowledge and entrepreneurial employees: A country-level analysis. *Small Business Economics, 41*(4), 887–898.

The U.S. Small Business Administration SBA.gov. (n.d.). Retrieved August 30, 2014, www.sba.gov

United States Patent and Trademark Office. (n.d.). Retrieved August 30, 2014, from http://www.uspto.gov/

Chapter 6

Aldrich, H., & Carter, N. (2004). Social networks. In *Handbook of Entrepreneurial Dynamics: The Process of Business Creation.* Thousand Oaks, CA: Sage, pp. 324–335.

American Express OPEN Survey. (n.d.). Retrieved from https://www.american-express.com/us/small-business/

Bhide, A. (1992). Bootstrap finance: The art of start-ups. *Harvard Business Review, 70*(6), 109–117.

Bitektine, A. (2011). Toward a theory of social judgments of organizations: The case of legitimacy, reputation, and status. *Academy of Management Review, 36*(1), 151–179.

De Carolis, D. M., Litzky, B. E., & Eddleston, K. A. (2009). Why networks enhance the progress of new venture creation: The influence of social capital and cognition. *Entrepreneurship Theory and Practice, 33*(2), 527–545.

Dess, G. G. (1987). Consensus on strategy formulation and organizational performance: Competitors in a fragmented industry. *Strategic Management Journal, 8*(3), 259–277.

Dodge, H. R., Fullerton, S., & Robbins, J. E. (1994). Stage of the organizational life cycle and competition as mediators of problem perception for small businesses. *Strategic Management Journal, 15*(2), 121–134.

Dollinger, M. J. (1990). The evolution of collective strategies in fragmented industries. *Academy of Management Review, 15*(2), 266–285.

Jones, O., & Jayawarna, D. (2010). Resourcing new businesses: Social networks, bootstrapping and firm performance. *Venture Capital, 12*(2), 127–152.

Moran, G. (2011, April 26). Business Incubators for a Variety of Niches. Retrieved August 30, 2014, from http://www.entrepreneur.com/article/219485

Ries, E. (2011). *The Lean Startup: How Today's Entrepreneurs Use Continuous Innovation to Create Radically Successful Businesses.* New York, NY: Random House LLC.

Rutherford, M. W., Buller, P. F., & Stebbins, J. M. (2009). Ethical considerations of the legitimacy lie. *Entrepreneurship Theory and Practice, 33*(4), 949–964.

Suchman, M. C. (1995). Managing legitimacy: Strategic and institutional approaches. *Academy of Management Review, 20*(3), 571–610.

Troutwine, C. (2011, January). Chad Troutwine of Veritas Prep [Video file]. Retrieved from http://www.entrepreneur.com/article/217619

Index

BABSON COLLEGE ENTREPRENEURSHIP RESEARCH CONFERENCE COLLECTION

Andrew "Zach" Zacharakis, Babson College, Editor

The Babson College Entrepreneurship Research Conference was founded by Babson College in 1981, and is considered by many to be the premier entrepreneurship research conference in the world. The Entrepreneurial Research Conference was established to provide a dynamic venue where academics and real-world practitioners, through spirited dialogue, could link theory and practice. Business Expert Press is proud to be affiliated with Babson and BCERC.

Other Titles In This Collection

- *Financing New Ventures: An Entrepreneur's Guide to Business Angel Investment* by Geoffrey Gregson

Business Expert Press and Andrew Zacharakis are actively seeking authors for this colleciton, as well as many others. For more information about becoming an BEP author, please visit http://www.businessexpertpress.com/contact.

Announcing the Business Expert Press Digital Library

Concise e-books business students need for classroom and research

This book can also be purchased in an e-book collection by your library as

- a one-time purchase,
- that is owned forever,
- allows for simultaneous readers,
- has no restrictions on printing, and
- can be downloaded as PDFs from within the library community.

Our digital library collections are a great solution to beat the rising cost of textbooks. E-books can be loaded into their course management systems or onto student's e-book readers.
The **Business Expert Press** digital libraries are very affordable, with no obligation to buy in future years. For more information, please visit www.businessexpertpress.com/librarians. To set up a trial in the United States, please contact **sales@businessexpertpress.com**.

CPSIA information can be obtained
at www.ICGtesting.com
Printed in the USA
LVOW01s0542140716

495681LV00014B/107/P